GODSPEED AND GUIDEPOSTS FOR YOUR JOURNEY

BOB MAHR

ISBN 978-1-64191-894-7 (paperback)
ISBN 978-1-64191-909-8 (hardcover)
ISBN 978-1-64191-895-4 (digital)

Christian Faith Publishing, Inc.
832 Park Avenue
Meadville, PA 16335
www.christianfaithpublishing.com

All Scriptures taken from New American Bible, Revised Edition (NABRE)

Printed in the United States of America

CONTENTS

Maybe you are getting this book as a graduation gift or at some important milestone in your life. This book can become a resource during a "hinge point" in your life between who you have been to date and who you will be. You are not leaving your old world behind; that experience has become a launching pad for the new world ahead of you. You should strive for continual growth throughout life. After all, life *is* a journey.

Look at these words of wisdom as guideposts along your journey. They are simple thoughts, sayings, and teachings that have impacted me over the years. They are lessons I learned from others along my journey. They have my spin on them. I think my catchphrases and analogies give them more stickiness and make them easier to recall. Enjoy this collection, and may God bless you on your journey.

Godspeed,
Coach Mahr

Prior to sharing my thoughts, it is important to share some background on the most influential person in my life—my Dad. His wisdom is included within all of this, because it was his wisdom that molded me. He had a basic and simple philosophy on life. There was nothing elaborate about his words or beliefs.

He taught me that success is extremely personal, telling me to define what it is and even what it is not. You will see the word success numerous times within these pages. Only you can define what success means to you; you set the criteria. Let those close to you guide and support you, but never let others decide if you are successful. Never judge your success against the success of others nor what someone, including me, describes in a book.

You will read about accountability and choices within this book. He made a choice during a "hinge point" in his life that was huge in changing the direction of his family. He took responsibility to make himself better and not be a victim of the prior generation defining the way for him. He never lost sight of making the world a better place for his family.

He created an environment in our home that allowed me, and my brothers, to grow and develop in a positive and confident way. His confidence in me created the foundation I had to build my life on.

It is true that choices have lasting impressions; they can alter the lives of people for generations.

This book is dedicated to his memory and legacy. Dad, I love you!

COACH MAHR'S
WORDS OF WISDOM

Introduction

Over the past thirty plus years during the formative part of my personal development, I have come to an understanding that thriving in life is kind of like sitting on a stool. A stool has a firm seat as a foundation, supported by three legs or "pillars."

My three pillars are "the Toothpaste Analogy," "Hope is Not Strategy," and "Do or Do Not; There is No Try," and the seat as a foundation is my all-time favorite quote from Father Pierre Teilhard de Chardin: "We are not human beings having a spiritual experience. We are spiritual beings having a human experience."

The pieces of the stool all work together and are required to make a stool complete as well as sturdy. Life is a sum total of many pieces all working together.

> *Life is one indivisible whole.*
> *—Mahatma Gandhi*

Pillar One: Toothpaste Analogy. If you squeeze a tube of toothpaste, what comes out? Toothpaste. Why? That is what was put in it in the first place. This is an easy analogy to see when you talk about food; an athlete who puts junk food into his/her body will play like junk. Consider an exam in high school or college which relies on the preparation made ahead of time. The toothpaste analogy also applies across life and temptation. When you find yourself in a pressure-packed situation and life squeezes you, what will come out? Whatever you have put in. If you have put in faith, character, morals, principles, then when you get squeezed, good will come out.

A wrong decision made in the heat of the moment is a result of a lack of preparation, conditioning, or putting quality toothpaste in the tube. There is an older expression that is similar to this concept that I once heard from my grandmother: "What is in the well comes up in the bucket." This harkens back to the days when people got their water from a well with a bucket. If there was polluted water in the well, then that's what came up in the bucket. There is also, in today's world, the computer acronym GIGO or "Garbage In Is Garbage Out," implying that the results are dependent upon the data that was entered.

Putting toothpaste in the tube is a form of mental conditioning. Just like running and lifting, you can condition yourself in this area. The more you practice, the better you become. The opposite also holds true. If you allow your mind to relax too much and get lazy and not take ownership, then it becomes more commonplace to just go through life letting circumstances control you, whether you recognize this control or not. The wonderful thing about sports and athletics is that the gym or the environment can develop the conditioning you will later need for life.

Pillar Two: Hope is Not a Strategy. *Hope* may be an action word, but it sets a low standard. I came across this adage while discussing an upcoming year's business strategy with a former boss (who also happened to be part owner of the company) when he said, "Let's hope our sales force takes action on our initiatives." I was caught off guard and replied that "hope is not a strategy, and I am not allowing my measure of achievement be tied to a hope that others do something not in my control." Hope is not a productive strategy to influence outcomes—i.e., hope I get the job, hope I pass this test, hope he/she likes me, hope this works out well.

Instead of using the word *hope* or even the word *faith*, I look to use the word *trust* if possible. Think about lending someone one hundred dollars. Do you *hope* they return it, have *faith* they return it, or *trust* they return it?

Hope is not sure of the outcome. The outcome could go either way, good or bad. Faith has no negative sides to it. Faith always believes in the eventual, ultimate outcome of the thing for which we believe. Strong faith is deeply rooted in trust. Trust comes by way of a relationship. Without trust, faith is often a thinly disguised hope. Faith is confidence. Your faith can waiver or even fail (Peter's denial of Jesus), and forces will work hard to cause you to lose your confidence. Trust is commitment; trust is eternal; it stands out and cannot be moved. When we trust God, we become like a mountain that cannot be moved (Psalm 125:1). Faith is something we *have*; trust is something we *do*. Faith says, "I believe." Trust is executing faith. It is far easier to have faith. It is a lot harder to exercise trust.

> *In leadership, there are no words more important than trust. In any organization, trust must be developed among every member of the team if success is going to be achieved.*
> —*Mike Krzyzewski, Hall of Fame*
> *College Basketball Coach*

Pillar Three: Do or Do Not; There is No Try. I use this expression so often around our house, it has become part of our everyday conversations. You probably know it comes from Yoda in the *Empire Strikes Back* movie of the *Star Wars* franchise. Own the outcome and the result even on those occasions you do not. Just to *try* is shirking ownership of the result. Since when did trying become good enough? One of my first lessons around trying was a sales job I had early in my career. We had Monday morning team meetings with a round table discussion on our activities, and every week, one guy kept telling our boss about all the appointments and sales he was trying to make. The boss finally snapped one Monday and said, "I don't pay you to try. I pay you to sell." I use that adage with my football players. When they tell me they tried to make that tackle they missed, I tell them I play kids who make the tackle as opposed to those who try to make it.

The word *try* has become more popular as we have become softer in our desire not to offend anyone, let alone fail them. One statement we usually hear is "as long as you tried, that is all that matters." Today, it is not politically correct to allow discomfort to ever develop. We associate failure with suffering, forgetting it is often how one learns to overcome and achieve. By congratulating the fact that one tried, we remove failure and how to respond to failure. We no longer develop the mindset to overcome problems or to persevere or to step up our efforts to meet the challenge.

We learn from our failures. Failure is part of success. As parents, my wife and I never wanted our daughters to fail, but we did look forward to their failures. Sometimes, what we learn when we are unsuccessful is the best education we can get. Many years ago, I owned a business that failed. It was a bump in the road that led to future successes. It may have been an expensive lesson but not a complete failure.

The Seat: Spiritual. "We are not human beings having a spiritual experience. We are spiritual beings having a human experience." This is my favorite quote, and it reminds me of why I exist. We are all children of God, a divine being. I see human beings acting upon the abilities and gifts God has bestowed, allowing His grace and beauty to shine through. A beautiful musical composition, an incredible sunset, and the birth of a child are moments we physically experience from within a spiritual existence. The spiritual realm existed long before the physical state. It exists today, and it will exist when the physical state is gone. It is all around us.

Compare our spiritual nature with our physical nature. We have the five physical senses (touch, sight, smell, taste, hear) which we share with other animals. But we also have the spiritual senses of thinking, feeling, and willing, which all separate us from animals. Our physical existence is a small part of our spiritual one. We should want to get the most out of our brief physical existence in a way that honors our spiritual essence.

TOOTHPASTE

How do we proactively put the right stuff into ourselves?

> *What lies behind us and what lies before us are*
> *tiny matters compared to what lies within us.*
> —*Oliver Wendell Holmes, Supreme Court Justice*

Actions are louder than words. Actions reflect your principles and beliefs. What you do, demonstrates what you believe and in turn what others do demonstrates their beliefs. Words (saying the right things) are easier than actions (doing the right things). Have your actions always match your words; by just doing that one thing, you will surpass many of those around you throughout your career and life.

Respect

Another principle is respect, specifically, respecting other's opinions and beliefs. Value what you have in common with someone as opposed to dwelling on your differences. When you respect someone else and their viewpoint, you allow yourself to learn from them. Learning from others is what allows you to keep growing. When we start discounting others, we become shallow minded which makes us want to listen less and further compounds the problem of respect—a doomed loop. Society today is inundated with many in this doomed loop.

Whether we respect someone else or not is a result of our behavior; it is our choice. It should not be dependent on the behavior of that individual. It is easy to respect a friend, mentor, or someone we get along with. It is harder to respect someone who disagrees with us.

Respect does not mean agreement. You can always agree to disagree. It is a combination of consideration and courage. Consideration is an element of respect; it is listening to others and taking to time to understand. Courage is being respectful to yourself and keeping true to your principles. Seek first to understand then be understood. This message is a two-way street; please don't confuse other's lack of agreement with you as a sign of disrespect.

Taking responsibility for our own existence implies respect for other people—the recognition that others do not exist simply to satisfy our needs. You cannot respect or trust yourself if you continually pass on to others the burdens of your existence.

The word origin of *competition* means "mutual quest for excellence"—a value-driven process that leads to respect for others, personal and team integrity, and justice and fairness. That is why the ancient Greeks invented the Olympics and the beginnings of organized sports—as well as the Native American Indians—to become better people and citizens. I think today's western society has skewed that original vision just a bit. It is important for athletes of all levels, as they move into the working world and the world at large, that they bring this "quest" with them.

The definition of *respect* is a "feeling of deep admiration for someone or something elicited by their abilities, qualities, or achievements." This definition bothers me. Achievements, qualities, and abilities as defined by the secular world around us are needed for respect? Really? Then the definition of *dignity* notes "state or quality of being worthy of respect." So following that logic, to have dignity, one must have abilities or achievements? Wrong!

Respect is man-given. However, respect is also God-demanded. Every person has a God-given dignity that can't

> I witnessed a funeral procession of cars where a gentleman, total stranger to the deceased, got out of his car and bowed his head as the cars went by. When asked why he did that for someone he didn't know, his answer was "Since when do you have to know someone to pay them respect?"

be taken away. Catholic social teaching states that every person has value and is worthy of profound respect, not because of what they may have done or what their title is or how much they are worth, but because they are a human being. Remember that we are all made in God's image, so whatever you do to the least of your brothers you do to God.

Self-Worth

> *If you put a small value upon yourself, rest assured that the world will not raise your price.*
> *—Unknown*

Satan's formula for self-worth is:

Self-Worth = Performance + Opinion of Others

This comes from Robert S. McGee's book titled *the Search for Significance.* If you are basing how valuable you are on the material results you obtain and what others think of you, then you will never recognize your true value unless you change this perspective first. You are letting your value be determined by others and things you can't control. This definition will lead to lying or embellishing as you will want to make yourself more valuable in the eyes others. You end up living a false life.

The world system prefers to define us not by who we are but by what we do, which is backwards. Instead, what we do should flow from who we are. While "doing" and "being" are related, it is the order they come in that is critical. If you define yourself by what you have done in the way of material achievements and accomplishments, then you place your self-worth (value) in the hands of others, particularly those who recognize and award these types of things. Our relationship with God has a foundation with time spent with Him not necessarily of what we do outwardly for Him (although that is the icing on the cake). A Christian who tries hard to please God will go to church, read the Bible, engage in religious activity, and could be focused more on "what we do" than "who we are."

God's promise to us is "His unconditional love" where performance and opinion by others has no bearing on who we are. In fact, putting any weight on performance and the opinion of others devalues God's promise.

> *Use what talents you possess: The woods would be very silent if no birds sang there except those that sang best.*
>
> *—Henry Van Dyke, American Author*

A key point of self-worth is that we cannot provide positive value for others if we don't value ourselves. Helping others when we have a low self-esteem lends itself to the martyr syndrome or "superman complex" and again places our own value on things external to us. Some people have low self-worth because they want people to feel sorry for them, to pay attention to them, to comfort them. Low self-esteem can be a declaration of "look at me" just as much as boastful pride. It simply takes a different route to get to the same destination, that is, self-absorption and selfishness.

I like the analogy taken from Scripture and the soundtrack from *Godspell* "Light of the World." The verse discusses being a candle, but if that candle is under a bushel, it's lost something kind of crucial. So be a bright raging flame as opposed to a faint glimmer of one.

> *Be who God meant you to be and you will set the world on fire.*
>
> *—St. Catherine of Siena, Third Order Dominican, Philosopher and Theologian*

Character

What makes up character? Your mindset, your thoughts, your choices, your actions, and your principles all form your character. It is the track record of what you have done to date—good or bad. It is your footprint.

> *Be more concerned with your character than your reputation, because your character is what you really are, while your reputation is merely what others think you are.*
> *—John Wooden, Hall of Fame College Basketball Coach and Author*

Character and integrity are intimately related. Character is the sum of qualities reflected in a person or group, moral or ethical strength, and the description of a person's attributes, traits, and abilities. Character is who you are. It defines you and guides your actions, ideally in a positive way.

Integrity can be summed up simply as doing the right thing for the right reason even when no one is watching. Again, strive to have integrity in the moment of choice. Integrity is steadfast adherence to a strict moral or ethical code, unimpaired, solid, whole, and undivided completeness. Our words and deeds match each other. The word *integrity* comes from the Latin word meaning "whole" or "complete," as in, whole number (integer).

Integrity is a foundation for a high-trust environment. Integrity comes first. No exceptions. Above winning. Above friendship. Above everything. Without integrity, credibility is lost, and trust cannot be built and maintained. Your credibility rises and falls with your integrity and trust.

Trustworthiness is at the center of people giving you the respect you deserve and responsibility you earn. If you lose the trust of others, it is hard to be productive in the long term and achieve your vision.

The wonderful thing about character and integrity is that they are one of the few things in life that no one will ever be able to forcefully take away from you. You choose to give them away. Strive to have integrity in the moment of choice. Choose based on your principles and values and not on your moods and temporary conditions.

> *Reputation is what men and women think of us; character is what God and angels know of us.*
> *—Thomas Paine, author of* Common Sense

Attitude

> *Nothing can stop the man with the right mental attitude from achieving his goal; nothing on earth can help the man with the wrong mental attitude.*
> *—Thomas Jefferson, US President*

I have seen repeatedly over the years people with the best attitude become the best students, best employees, and the people that I want to be around. I have made hiring decisions based on an individual's attitude over and above than their talents. Surround yourself with friends and colleagues who believe in themselves. A positive and can-do attitude stems from an elevated level of self-worth. I am not sure where I heard this, but I have used it frequently in the past few years coaching football, and it also applies to business management—"I can only alter your mood. You must change your attitude."

Change comes from inward out. Author Stephen Covey writes private victories precede public victories. All things created begin in the mind. Consider music or a building; they both started as mental inspirations. It is the same with your personal nature—it begins in your mind with your thoughts.

How you think leads to the choices you make and the habits you develop. All of that creates the person you become. If how one thinks determines who and what they become, then attitude is in fact "a manner of thinking." To take it one more step, if "attitude is everything" and "our attitude determines our altitude," then what we are saying is that we have got to improve our "manner of thinking." Like the toothpaste, what goes into our thinking comes out in our attitude.

As founder of the local county AAU basketball program, I felt so strongly about attitude and the role it plays in any successful team effort (sports, work, or community) that I named the program "Attitude." It is my belief that young girls, who play for the Attitude, and their parents understand this key point.

> *Nurture your mind with great thoughts, for you will never go any higher than you think.*
> —*Benjamin Disraeli, Prime Minister of England*

Discipline Is Not a Bad Word

We have a sign in our football locker room. "Discipline is not what we do *to* you, it is what we do *for* you." As a high school football coach, an unexpected requirement of the job is to convince young men that discipline is not a bad word. Until that point in their life for most, discipline has become synonymous with punishment. When they hear the word *discipline* from a football coach, they envision endless wind sprints or up/downs.

Even the dictionary definition paints that picture—the practice of training people to obey rules or a code of behavior, using punishment to correct disobedience.

Discipline is really a positive exercise around choice. It not only prevents negative consequences (that bad stuff like time out as a 3-year-old or those dreaded wind sprints), but more importantly, it makes good stuff better and prepares yourself or your team for the challenges ahead. It is a good thing that enriches you. When discipline is imposed from the outside (a coach, parent, manager), it will eventually wane and dissipate when there is no desire to match from within.

There is the conscious part of discipline; it is the mindfulness and awareness to self-regulate. Managing our own thoughts, feelings, and actions is the cornerstone of a positive life. If you are an effective manager of yourself, your discipline comes from within. Most people can prioritize and even organize around their priorities; how-

23

ever, many lack discipline to choose and execute according to their priorities.

> *Self-respect is the root of discipline; the sense of dignity grows with the ability to say no to oneself.*
> *—Abraham Joshua Heschel, Jewish Theologian and Philosopher*

Discipline is the bridge between goals and accomplishments; discipline takes you from wishing for accomplishments to achieving them. You cannot just talk your way to long-term success; you need to discipline yourself with action to make it happen.

> *We must all suffer from one of two pains: the pain of discipline or the pain of regret. The difference is discipline weighs ounces while regret weighs tons.*
> *—Jim Rohn, American Author and Motivational Speaker*

Making better mental choices (accountable choices) requires mental discipline. Mental discipline is essential to the process of winning, especially in times of uncertainty (change). Mental discipline is key to finishing what you start.

Aesop's fable of the ant versus the grasshopper is centered on discipline. The ant is symbolic of discipline with diligence in its approach to life—storing food for winter, working as part of a colony and supporting others. The grasshopper is carefree and overly individualistic, lacking in self-discipline.

Note that being obedient is not the same as being disciplined. Obedience is following the rules, meeting deadlines, and checking the boxes that you did what you were supposed to do (being compliant). Discipline is more than following rules. It is about doing the right thing (there is no rule that says if you used the last of the toilet paper, put on a new roll), about living a code of accountability to exceed expectations and being "excellent."

It was interesting to learn that the original Greek word used for discipline is also where we get the English word *gymnasium*. Training, practice, discipline—all are required for success in sports, in work, and in life.

Any individual can dole out the punishment form of discipline, especially someone in a leadership position. However, true leaders strive to provide understanding and to actively help deal with the larger issue that resulted in the mistake leading up to punishment. Modeling a disciplined life is far more effective than correcting disobedience. Honoring your word every day is discipline mentoring in its simplest form.

The words *discipline* and *disciple* share the same root word, *discipulus*, which is Latin for "pupil." The concept is that we surrender ourselves to something or someone, like an athlete surrendering his will to a coach or a student to her teacher. As disciples, our surrender is given to God and His wisdom. Every disciple of Christ must practice discipline as we "train yourself for devotion" (1 Timothy 4:7). Proverbs of Solomon is written for us to gain discipline for wise conflict management "that people may know wisdom and discipline, may understand intelligent sayings; May receive instruction in wise conduct, in what is right, just and fair" (Proverbs 1:2–3). Solomon also said that we should love discipline. "Whoever loves discipline loves knowledge, but whoever hates rebuke is stupid" (Proverbs 12:1).

Referencing back to Aesop and the ant: "Go to the ant, O sluggard, observe her ways and be wise, which, having no chief, officer or ruler, prepares her food in the summer and gathers her provision in the harvest." (Proverbs 6:6–8).

Reflective Mindfulness and Awareness

Part of a reflective mindset is engaging with yourself in private conversations. It is important that you have these conversations with "respect of self." I believe this is one of the biggest shortcomings with too many in our young generation. First, that generation does not engage in reflective thought enough. Second, it does not respect itself when being self-critical.

Today's world is one of constant communication, always on electronic devices and social networking. There is this need to be in constant touch with others. It creates that state of being in the "thick of thin things." Losing real relationships with others and God.

Do we take time to talk to God, pray, reflect, or even sit quietly with nature? The Nike slogan of "don't just sit there, do something" needs to be reversed "don't just do something, sit there"—and reflect or discern!

> *Do not conform yourselves to this age but be trans-formed by the renewal of your mind, that you may discern what is the will of God, what is good and pleasing and perfect.*
>
> *—Romans 12:2,*

To "discern" is to perceive with intellect or comprehend mentally. It is important to perceive and detect the spiritual elements of life—remember, we are human beings but we are also spiritual beings.

Looking is not the only important aspect of a search; to find what you are looking for requires that you look in the right direction. We must also look in the right manner, with a reflective mindset.

> *Keep your head and your heart going in the right direction and you will not have to worry about your feet.*
>
> —*Unknown*

Mindfulness is an attentive awareness of the reality of things, especially of the present moment. It keeps thing real. By having mindfulness in one's day-to-day life, one maintains a calm awareness of one's body and movements, feelings, thoughts, and perceptions.

What creates much of your mindset and how you can make choices is awareness. Awareness is habits that are learned. You might hear the expression "its second nature," meaning it is a habit that has been developed, not something that is instinctive. Habits can become unlearned or relearned, allowing you to break unhealthy habits and start new good habits.

Awareness is a self-sustaining aspect. The more you practice it, the more aware you become of your surroundings—nature, friend-

One of my favorite respites is the family annual camping vacation, which is a break to experience nature and quiet time. We enjoy the early morning stillness, coffee, looking out over the lake, a brisk hike through the woods, and the opportunity to peacefully reflect.

ship, kindness, and little things. Being aware of God in the present moment is a great comfort and inspiration. Your conscience is your awareness barometer.

> *The voice of conscience is so delicate that it is easy to stifle it; but it is also so clear that it is impossible to mistake it.*
> —*Madame de Stael, French Political Activist*

Awareness in hindsight is far easier than awareness in the present. However, awareness of what the past has transpired can strengthen awareness of what is happening today.

I read an analogy once that your conscience can serve like rumble strips do on a highway—God's little nudges to keep you on the road.

Being aware is a huge challenge for a young adult. The world has been relatively small, at least smaller than it will become. It has been structured, with routine and control built in. College, jobs, and the real world are larger, more dynamic, and complex. Your level of awareness will be challenged to grow. If you do not build your capabilities in awareness, life will be more challenging and probably more expensive.

Moses was no one special, had no particular gifts. It was his awareness of God's presence that awakened him to many wonderful things. Another fitting example from the Bible on awareness is Elijah. To him, God appeared in the whisper, not the earthquake nor the fire.

I have had my own experience of "hearing the whisper." One experience I still remember very vividly, and from it, I draw comfort. Many years ago, within a week after my dad had passed away, I was looking for his electrical tape. I had been looking for a while, getting a bit frustrated. So, I paused, relaxed, and asked out loud, "Dad, where would the tape be?" And immediately, I moved to open the drawer where it was.

A big aspect of awareness that has helped me to create balance is identifying and understanding my roles in life. A great exercise is to identify all your roles then look at them in total. This gives an on paper look at your life which will give some sense and order to it. When I identified the roles of husband, dad, son, brother, son-in-law, brother-in-law, uncle, coach, neighbor, friend, employee, etc., it allowed me to be aware of who I was on many levels. I was then able to see how they related and how I could prioritize and find balance. It added control to my life and clarified the choices I could make. This is a whole lot better than just running from one thing to the next allowing life to control me. Balance is not *either/or*; it is *and*.

Little Things

In your daily routine of experiencing life, you want to pay attention to the little things. They can make a significant difference. We often have more input and choice over how we handle the small things in life. Throw a tiny pebble into a pond, and the entire pond surface will have ripples of waves across it. A horse with a bit can plow a field; a ship with a rudder can deliver goods and people across an ocean; a person with an empathetic tongue can share love, compassion, and kindness.

Consider patient zero of the AIDS epidemic; this one individual's actions created a worldwide epidemic. There were those first stink bugs that made their way to Allentown, PA, and now look at them everywhere in the mid-Atlantic states. Rain changes to snow or water to steam in the difference of one degree. Paul Revere's ride was one man's action that rallied a nation.

> *Sometimes when I consider what tremendous consequences come from little things… I am tempted to think there are no little things.*
> —*Bruce Barton, American Author and Congressman*

The difference between success and failure is often a very small margin. Two people with virtually the same amount of skill and talent can differ vastly in the amount of success they achieve. You don't have to be ten times or twenty times or a hundred times better than the next person. You can simply be slightly better to achieve remarkable results. In the world of professional golf, less than a stroke per round separates the top player from the fiftieth best player. Yet, this stroke difference is millions of dollars in winnings.

> *Four short words sum up what has lifted most successful individuals above the crowd: a little bit more. They did all that was expected of them and a little bit more.*
> —*Lou Vickery, Former Professional Baseball Player*

In Matthew 5:41, we read a common phrase in our English language: "Should anyone press you into service for one mile, go with him for two miles." Jesus is talking about testimony, about "going the extra mile." At that time in history, a Roman citizen could approach anyone in the conquered territory to commandeer their time and effort. That person was "compelled to go one mile." But Jesus was saying "Do 'a little bit more!'"

It is important to appreciate life's little things—a smile, a hug, a song bird chirping, a sunset. It is also important to do the little things—say hello to someone you pass in the halls or on campus, hold the door open for a person walking in behind you, a hug for no reason.

Rushing through the day to accomplish all those big tasks, we become blind to the nonverbal signs of God working in our lives. God's presence is in the trivial things, the ordinary things in daily life. God works through the lives of ordinary people. History records the great names, but the mission moves forward through the acts of ordinary people. Who did Jesus call? Fishermen, laborers, tax collectors.

Be Happy

> *Success is not the key to happiness. Happiness is the key to success.*
> *—Albert Schweitzer, Theologian, Philosopher*

We talk about choosing to be happy, but it is really a key component to being successful. Happy and positive people look for ways to be successful and create their opportunities; negative people look for ways to complain and create their own misery.

Is the glass half full or half empty? I always say it is "half full with more milk in the fridge." Choose to be positive when dealing with others. Be a light shining a path for others and not a judge who sees shortcomings; be a model to emulate, not a critic who improves their standing by lowering the standing of others. Root for others to succeed; most people want to get better. Studies have shown that an individual's success is mostly based on whether one believes one will succeed.

Thomas Jefferson and our Founding Fathers included in our Declaration of Independence from England the phrase that "Life, Liberty and the pursuit of Happiness" are inalienable rights of man. Those words have also been included in the 1947 Constitution of Japan, the 1945 Declaration of the Independence of Vietnam, as well as in several Supreme Court rulings. The key point is that happiness is not a right, but the pursuit of it is. One should be free to pursue whatever it is that will provide him happiness.

> *The US Constitution doesn't guarantee happiness, only the pursuit of it. You have to catch up with it yourself.*
>
> *—Benjamin Franklin, Founding Father of the United States*

If you do not enjoy what you are doing, you are not going to be able to give it the diligence that it needs. It can spell the difference between mediocrity and accomplishment. In many cases, the more successful person had less ability. The difference is enthusiasm. Without enthusiasm, everything else becomes virtually powerless. Enthusiasm is the energy, the fuel, the blazing fire that brings about a successful result.

> *Nothing great was ever achieved without enthusiasm.*
> —*Ralph Waldo Emerson, Essayist, Lecturer, and Poet*

In the comparison between passion versus competence, always take passion. If a car has fuel but the driver does not know how to drive, he can learn or be coached. But if the car has no fuel, no matter how competent the driver, it is just going to sit there.

> *The credit belongs with the man who is actually in the arena, whose face is marred by dust and sweat and blood; who strives valiantly; who errs and comes short again and again, who knows the great* enthusiasms, *the great devotions, and spends himself in a worthy cause; who at the best, knows the triumph of high achievement; and who, at the worst, if he fails at least fails while daring greatly, so that his place shall never be with those cold and timid souls who know neither victory nor defeat.*
> —*Theodore Roosevelt, President, Author, Naturalist*

A problem is that most people wait to be enthusiastic about something. Unfortunately, enthusiasm does not come to us directly—it must be created. We must take responsibility for creating this enthusiasm in our lives. That is a choice we own.

Leave a Legacy

Leaving a legacy is a profound concept. Step outside your life for a moment and reflect upon what it will mean to others after you are gone. Whose life have you touched and in what way? It is very rewarding when you learn about how you impacted someone else.

> *What you leave behind is not what is engraved in stone monuments, but what is woven into the lives of others.*
> —*Pericles, Greek Statesman and Orator*

We discussed "leaving a legacy" as a topic for a character session before the final football game of a season. Ordinary things—days, events, people, etc.—without something noteworthy tied to them will fade from memory and become part of the blur. Outside of a handful of family and friends, it will never be remembered. What can't be remembered is forgotten; what is forgotten never gets deposited into our memory banks; what doesn't get deposited is that which does not strike a chord.

Extraordinary things are another story. There is no generic definition of extraordinary, noteworthy, or "big" that guarantees something becoming memorable. But one thing is for certain—to qualify, it must strike a chord. Anything that strikes a chord will be remembered longer than usual. If it really strikes a chord, we can remember it forever. Striking a chord is leaving a legacy. What qualifies as striking a chord is subject to the very personal, relative context where it occurs—the environment, background, situation, and perspective.

Winning the state championship does not necessarily make a team memorable or cause it to leave a legacy; the same with making

GODSPEED AND GUIDEPOSTS FOR YOUR JOURNEY

a big play or being a sports hero. As an example, a team with a 6-4 record left as big a legacy as the 12-1 state semifinalist team. That first team changed the culture of the football program, creating the foundation for the future team to build on.

It is important to note that success is not the standard for leaving a legacy—significance is. As Robin Sharma, author of twelve global best sellers, is quoted as saying "success is wonderful, but significance is even better." As individuals, we are created and put here to make a difference, contribute, and leave a mark on the people around us. Success is a standard of measurement in man's world, while significance is the standard in God's world.

My analogy of leaving a legacy is like the wake behind a boat. The wake that is left behind a boat exists because of the water moved by the boat, thus displaced. The wake (legacy) is there because of the boat (event, you) moved or displaced what was around you (others). What moves your mind, heart, or soul can leave a legacy within you. Consider a book you read, a movie you saw, or a song you heard that moved you—it left a legacy.

Consider the wake left behind an aircraft carrier—a lot of displacement occurs which creates a huge wake and a significant trail. We all have people in our lives who, like an aircraft carrier, leave a longer lasting legacy. There is a scene in the movie *Apollo 13* where actor Tom Hanks, who is playing astronaut Jim Lovell, talks about an experience he had with the wake of an aircraft carrier. He was a Navy pilot coming back from a mission, and he has lost all guidance, and his radio had

> A notable example for me is Jim Valvano's 1993 ESPY speech in total just eleven minutes and thirty-six seconds; but powerful and significant.

35

no way to find the aircraft carrier. Just when he thought things were bad enough, it got worse as he lost all electricity in the cockpit—it went dark. He is sitting there alone, lost, and surrounded by total darkness. It is then he sees the wake of the aircraft carrier—because of the volume of displacement and the ocean having been churned, it had a fluorescent glow that could only be seen because he was in total darkness. It was the legacy left from something so voluminous which caused significant movement that it became the guiding path to someone lost and in darkness. How is that for an analogy for Christ!

Historians tell us that two plagues swept through the Roman Empire in the first couple of centuries after the life of Christ, both while Christians were horribly persecuted. The second of these was the Plague of Cyprian where one document states that, in Rome, as many as five thousand were dying per day. The epidemic filled the people with terror. It was so devastating that when the first symptoms appeared, some villages simply were deserted, leaving the sick behind. There was no cure. There was no hope. They left sick family members in their beds and many who could run ran for their lives.

But Christians did not run. They stayed and brought water to the sick. They fed them. They changed their bandages. They spoke kindly to them. They loved and encouraged them. And some got sick themselves in the process.

Jesus would not have left the sick to fend for themselves; so in effect, these Christians did what Jesus would have done. There is no record of how many people were saved from these selfless acts nor how many Christians lost their lives because they stayed behind. But the world is different today because in the middle of devastating despair—some might even call it overwhelming darkness—those who followed Christ saw their opportunity to let God shine through them. The community in and around this village could not ignore the actions of these early Christians who loved God so passionately that they would be willing to give up their own lives in service to God. They left a legacy that Jesus began, one of love-filled action that leads to salvation. This is one major reason why the Roman Empire changed so dramatically. Emperor Constantine ended the persecution of Christians and inspired the growth of a Christian ruling class under Constantine which ensured the faith's increasing and enduring prominence throughout the Roman and later Byzantine Empire.

Be intentional about leaving a legacy. Create displacement to those around you, even with what seem like small acts. To someone else, it may be a huge act of love. Build your legacy by adding value to everyone you encounter and leaving the world a better place in the process. Your legacy is putting your stamp on the future. It's a way to make some gratifying meaning of your own existence: "Yes, world of the future, I was here. Here's my contribution. Here's why my life mattered."

HOPE IS NOT A STRATEGY

How do we move beyond the concept of placing control on outcomes outside of our own reach?

We use the story of a tightrope walker in the FCA Huddle, a fellowship study group, to further clarify the concept of faith and trust. In the late 1800s, there was a great tightrope walker. One of his greatest stunts involved walking a tightrope high above the world-famous Niagara Falls. Upon completing one attempt, he asked the crowd if they believed he could do it again. The crowd agreed. Looking to go one better, he asked if they believed he could cross while pushing a wheelbarrow. The crowd had no doubt he could pull this off. Right as he started he asked, "Which of you will ride in the wheelbarrow?" No one responded. They had faith he could perform the more difficult stunt. Yet, when it came time to act on those beliefs, they did not trust him.

Life, like most team sports (football, basketball, hockey), can be fast moving. A lot happens in seconds with little time to think. Everything that a player has learned in practice needs to come out naturally and automatically. Athletes improve their performances tremendously by learning and playing with trust. Trust is letting go of the mental need to control. When you have trust in your own ability to perform the task in competition, you play in a "flow state" where your full talent manifests. In coaching an AAU basketball player, my thought was that she "has a good shot but doesn't trust it," and eventually, she never really became the player she could have been. To develop trust, you must first eliminate the main block to it: fear—failure, mistakes, opinion by others, results, injury, etc.

Goal Setting

Along with setting realistic expectations, you need to set goals. Goals can be long term or short term; they can be smaller goals that build to a larger goal. The key is to make them *SMART* goals. Make them specific—not general. Make them measurable—so you know how you stand against the goal. Make them attainable—something you have control over and can achieve. Make them relevant—something appropriate and meaningful to you. And all within a defined time frame.

> *The tragedy of life doesn't lie in not reaching your goal. The tragedy lies in having no goal to reach.*
> —*Benjamin Mays, American Minister and Civil Rights Icon*

One of the best examples of goal setting I have ever encountered was the goal by NASA to put a man on the moon. Prior to John Kennedy's famous speech in May of 1961, the stated goal of NASA was "to achieve maximum effectiveness in space." How does that goal compare with the SMART guidelines? It is not specific, measurable, nor tied to any time frame. Now, in JFK's speech, he stated, "We will put a man on the moon and return him safely to earth before the end of the decade." That is certainly specific, measurable, attainable (although many doubted it was at the time), relevant to the needs of the country, and within a defined time frame. History shows this goal was achieved and a remarkable accomplishment for NASA and our country—at a time when our nation's morale needed it.

Fighter pilot Scott O'Grady spoke at a convention I attended. He was shot down over Bosnia behind enemy lines in June 1995. Sharing his life experience at that event, he talked about goal setting and how it played a key role in his staying alive and avoiding capture. He survived for six days alone by setting specific goals for the day. Every day goal #1 was to stay alive and remain free. Then he set smaller goals like putting distance away from where his parachute landed, finding water, finding food, climbing as high as possible to communicate by radio, heading to a cleared area for rescue, etc. He said that by breaking everything down into smaller SMART goals, he could stay focused. If he had looked at the whole picture of his dire situation and tried to comprehend a total solution, he would have been overwhelmed by it all and likely would have been captured.

It is important to remember you do not win a game all at once and never in the first few minutes. It is played out in small increments. So is life. Success is more of a marathon than it is a sprint.

You will not be able to accomplish everything you want. It is just impossible given a finite amount of time. So, you will need to triage your goals. Prioritize. What survives becomes the focus and other things are left to wither away. Realizing that time is a finite resource, and by having a plan and guide posts to live by, allows you to align your time against what is important. Some things in life cost time, some cost money, and some cost both. Decide what is important enough to spend time on. Some call this the "Law of Releasing"—

you must get rid of what you do not necessarily want to make room for what you really do want.

By prioritizing your goals and planning around those priorities, you determine what is most important. Do not get lost in the thick of thin things. Please do not allow for unimportant, nonurgent activities to consume any more than one percent of your time. Life is too sacred and valuable to waste it.

> *Things which matter most should never be at the mercy of things which matter least.*
> —*Johann Wolfgang von Goethe,*
> *German Write and Statesman*

Be flexible. You will most likely revisit your goals and your plan with the need to adjust. Remember that you can correct your journey's path as you move along it. Striving to stick with the exact path you lay out can be difficult, and there will be things you cannot control that will cause you to adapt. The analogy is that of a strong wind blowing, and that which is rigid will snap and break. Those things that are flexible will bend with the wind. When the winds die down and calm returns, the flexible will rise again.

Align your professional goals with your personal goals and not the other way around. Your personal goals are your foundation, and the professional goals need to be what gets intertwined and reconciled against that foundation. A key to finding balance is having one side as the basis to balance against (personal) and only adjusting the other side (professional) as opposed to adjusting both sides.

Relationships are also like goals in that you do not have time for everyone. Give up relationships that do not enhance your life of becoming a better person. The same way you triage goals, you must triage relationships. You can just as easily get sucked into the thick of thin things with people. Identify those relationships that are most important. Leave relationships that drag you down, but you do not walk away from responsibilities that are your core, such as family and dear friends who need your support. This step of triaging relationships is made more difficult if you have placed the value of self-worth in their hands. As you get older, your circle of acquaintances and friends expands; this "triage" concept becomes more valuable.

Live in Your Vision, Not Your Circumstance; Trust the Process

Too many times, we as individuals "live in circumstances," instead of "living in a vision." We are all human, and often, we focus on what we don't have instead of what can be. How many people live in circumstances and complain about the election, their boss, or complain about all the

> I have always said that I am talented enough to find another job or employer, but I will not find another family or personal life that is as blessed as the one I have.

things that didn't go their way or what they don't have? We all have difficult circumstances in our lives. There are dozens of problems (circumstances) we encounter every day which can lead us to focus only on the negative side of life. We then blame our unhappiness on our circumstances, which fuels the feeling of being powerless over our lives.

It's our thinking, not our circumstances, that determines how we feel. We are in charge of our thinking; we are the ones doing

42

the thinking—then why should circumstances be dictating our experience of life? We cannot control the circumstances that we may encounter, but we can control how we react to those circumstances. Controlling our reactions takes mental conditioning; you need to cultivate it, and it grows with practice. Circumstances are temporary. A vision can last an eternity. If you have a vision, nothing can stop you. Make that conscious decision and start living your vision, not someone else's. In response to challenging circumstances, winners consciously choose accountability over "victimhood."

Living in your vision is imperative to staying the course when surrounded by circumstances and disruptions. If you don't have a good, solid vision, get one. And live in it. Everyone needs a dream. I also refer to a "vision" as the *what*. What do you want your life to look like or your story to be? If you don't have a powerful answer to the *why* (your purpose), you can easily get caught up in the circumstances, be distracted, lose your way, or even worse, easily be enticed back into the safety of the known, doing little or nothing.

The second part of this principle after "live in your vision, not in your circumstance" is "trust the process." Where there's a vision, as I also referred to it as a *what*, there needs to be a process of the *how*. A "vision" implies you have a mental view of your end goal, but it doesn't necessarily mean you know exactly the best path which will get you there. There are lots of roads. Some of the roads may turn out to be dead ends, but there's always another road to take. When we have a vision and believe in it, we see the discovery and growth amidst the daily grind and maybe even the chaos. Once we know our why (purpose) and what (vision), there will be a how. We've got to trust the process in the day to day.

The "Law of the Harvest" principle applies to life. You need to plant in the spring, tend the weeds, water, control birds and pests if you expect to have a harvest in the fall. You can't dismiss the natural processes and cram all the steps in at the end. However, society promotes us to take short cuts, maybe even cheat the system. We then desire to "want it now" with an immediate gratification mindset.

Being disciplined in your approach to each day of your life and accomplishing your dreams starts by disciplining your thoughts. If you live out your vision, then you tend to focus on those things that you want to occur, whereas living amongst your circumstance focuses on what has not occurred or will not occur. You will never be able to rise above the imaginary ceiling you construct in your mind.

Stress and Worry

When you consider the element of choice, it makes stress neither positive nor negative. Stress is a response, and your choice makes it positive or negative. Life deals us stressful situations. How we manage those situations is what counts. This is easier said than done and, again, is one of those areas that will grow with conditioning. Choose your response to life's situations such that you do not feel stress or at least recognize that your reaction is causing the stress.

> *Pressure is something that you feel only when you don't know what you are doing.*
> *—Chuck Noll, Hall of Fame Football Coach*

In understanding choice, know that you always have the choice to say no. Saying no can mean saying yes. We have a finite amount of time in a day and enough energy to accomplish what we want to do. If you spend all your time and energy responding to the continuous requests of others, then you are prevented from spending it in the way you want. Make sure you are not pleasing others just to meet their deadlines. Avoid that needy "superhero" complex, the unconscious need to be wanted all the time, thinking that it is helpful. When you are active for yourself by your choice, it is rewarding and fulfilling. When you are active for others, you can become resentful and feel overwhelmed.

> *A no uttered from the deepest conviction is better than a yes merely uttered to please, or what is worse, to avoid trouble.*
> *—Mahatma Gandhi, Social*
> *Activist and Spiritual Leader*

I attended a sales training once that was built around "going for the no," which is a highly unusual tactic for sales where you would think you would always want to "go for the yes." The philosophy is that if you can quickly identify those situations where you have no chance or little chance of getting a sale, you can move on and spend time where you have a quality chance for a sale.

Worrying, like stress, is also a choice that you have control over and can choose to eliminate if you so wish. In some cases, worry becomes a habit. All worry does is steal time and energy that can be invested somewhere else. In Matthew 6:27, Jesus asked, "Can any of you, by worrying, add a single moment to your life span?" God's plan does not include worry, because worry eats at faith. If you truly have God in your life, then you should not worry. I saw a bumper sticker years ago, that said: "If your problem is too big, your God is not big enough."

> *I've noticed that worrying is like praying for what you don't want to happen.*
> —*Robert Downey Jr., American Actor (yes,* Iron Man*)*

Being a realist, I recognize that eliminating all stress and worry is nearly impossible. In fact, a small level of "tension" in your life can be a catalyst for growth. Look at this as the tension in a rubber band. If there is too much tension (you pull too hard), it snaps, and you become burnt out. If there is no tension at all, it sags, and you become complacent. Again, how you deal with the issues of life determines how much stress, anxiety, and pressure you "self-inflict."

Train for Excellence

The Navy Seals have an adage that says something very similar—"Under pressure, you don't rise to the occasion; you sink to the level of your training. That's why we train for excellence." I read this in a Harvard Business Review article debating the business merits of training versus education. The failure of so many smart and talented organizations to innovate and adapt under pressure can be a result of overeducation and undertraining. The failure of strategies developed by the high-priced consultant or based on the theory from top business schools are blamed on the lack of execution and talent of the personnel, when in reality, it is the lack of proper training. Businesses tend to train for competence, not excellence.

I have also seen this adage with high school football players. When it gets tough late in the game and mistakes are more noticeable because players are tired, the pressure to perform well is at its highest.

Young athletes believe they will rise to the occasion. "Trust me coach, I'll make that play." However, it is only the players who have trained at the peak level who can deliver that kind of result.

What is not obvious is that the lack of specific training for excellence will cause similar issues in your faith and life situations when there is greater pressure. Do we train for excellence regarding executing our faith journey such that when we are placed in a stressful situation or temptation catches us off guard, we can rise to the occasion? Are we complacent in our training, checking off the box of Sunday service, focusing on good enough, seeking the minimum rather than excellence? Jesus spent hours in prayer as his training for excellence. He spent forty days in the wilderness, tempted in preparation for his calling.

Training for excellence is about transformation, not just incremental improvement. Never settle for good enough or getting slightly better. Set the highest internal standard for yourself and train to reach that goal. It takes discipline to train for excellence, and you will not see the results in common day-to-day performance. It will be at a time when it matters most, and maybe when least expected, that you will bear the fruits of your efforts. Put the best toothpaste in the tube that you can.

Be Exceptional

You are exceptional, one of a kind in God's eyes, so be exceptional. Be unique. Be something that does not conform to a pattern or the norm. The norm is not exceptional; the norm is falling back into the crowd and blending in. Some even think they are doing a good thing by blending in and not calling attention to themselves. We all have been given the gift of uniqueness. We need to accept and nurture that gift in ourselves and others. You know you are exceptional when others "level set" you, because when they do a compari-son, they realize they do not have your uniqueness, and to overcome their lack of self-worth, they feel they must discount you and your unique gift.

"Being exceptional" means you must live out the word *except*. Everyone complains about the coach (boss, manager, parents, teacher, etc.), except me; everyone is walking around offended by something, except me; I was at a party where people were getting high or drunk, except me. To be exceptional, you must make a choice that even though others do that stuff, it is not for you. Choose what matters to you, what makes you feel exceptional. You can be exceptional, but you must live this statement, "They all did that, believed that, said that, except me." Don't mimic your environment of today or yes-terday. Don't be of it, but be above it. Rise above the crowd and be unique because you are exceptional. Be an eagle and soar.

Being exceptional is not superior nor arrogant. It does not mean you are better than anybody else. It means that you are going to con-sciously, daily, be driven by a choice, not a feeling. I am attempting to be exceptional by not being offended. So many people live their days angry, because they feel offended. I have found that choosing to not be offended has made me happier.

God gave each of us the gifts that we need to do the specific job He has in mind for us to do. You were made unique for a unique job. Maybe in your eyes, it's not a glamorous job, but to Him, it is everything. You cannot do the job that someone else does as you do not have their gifts, but someone else cannot do yours either.

The cause of much misery is the self-comparison to others. Most people will tell you that they are stressed out, but indeed they are just "offended," and the anger at being offended causes a lack of ease. They want to blame this offended feeling on someone (other than themselves) so they call it stress. Comparison on a continuous basis will always make you think that what others are doing and receiving is taking away from you.

God did not create you to run *against* others but rather to run *with Him* in your heart and head. God did not create you to blend in and get lost in the masses. Cherish the gifts you have received—that which God put inside of you to make you unique and exceptional—and be grateful.

By comparing, you are making a statement: "Who I am and what I have are not enough." You are making others your benchmark, not you yourself and your blessings or gifts. Comparison is also a scarcity mentality when you want an abundance mentality. Life is not a win-lose game. There is enough of His abundance that we are all winners.

> *But you know in life we're called upon to do things. A Ford car trying to be a Cadillac is absurd, but if a Ford will accept itself as a Ford, it can do many things that a Cadillac could never do: it can get in parking spaces that a Cadillac can never get in. And in life some of us are Fords and some of us are Cadillacs.*
>
> *—Martin Luther King, Baptist Minister and Civil Rights Activist*

Some people do not want to have who they consider exceptional people around, because in those people's own eyes, it devalues themselves. Some aspects of society (i.e. socialism) emphasize being the norm. We see that in our culture today with high school honor societies having lowered standards, giving all teams that participate a medal, allowing all students to pass a class. Broadening the definition of excellence placates the norm and reduces exceptionalism.

There is the story of how fellow engineers and artisans lambasted Gustave Eiffel, the designer of the Eiffel Tower, for his effort to be exceptional. They protested with indignation against building it, calling it useless and monstrous. They ridiculed his lack of imagination and creativity. Today, the Eiffel Tower is the most visited paid monument in the world.

We move from being accomplished to exceptional through the power of discontent within ourselves. That dissatisfaction is a good thing. We no longer tolerate being accomplished and want to be part of something more meaningful and powerful. We seek to be challenged, so we are part of a bigger story.

Like a brilliantly aged wine and cheese, it takes time and stubborn consistency to be exceptional as a person, a group, a society, and as a nation. In other words, you do not stumble into being exceptional.

Feet and Courage to Meet in the Aisle

We have become a society more concerned with our side, our viewpoint, our philosophies, and that we are right or that we win and the other side is wrong or they lose. It is a shame that in today's world, the investment of time and effort is focused on proving ourselves right or winning the debate with little to none spent on understanding the other side or even the greater good. This type of behavior is not limited to politics. Daily, it is reflected in commentary about race, religion, and society in general.

At the end of the day, are we getting better? As my college football coach used to say, "If we are not getting better (moving forward), we are getting worse (moving backwards)." How can we collectively get better when we work almost one hundred percent against the other side? This is scarcity mentality at its best—if I don't win, I lose.

When we see our side as right and our position as the norm, how do we collectively move forward? Do we consider our actions to engage others as reaching out, or do we view it as reaching down to help others up? Better yet, do we even extend a hand? The expression "reaching across the aisle" in politics is plain hogwash. If you take it at its words, it means we have kept our feet firmly planted where we stand. Why do we not literally meet between the aisles, causing us both to move somewhat?

Imagine that you have a piece of string between your two hands and consider it an analogy for moving something forward. Pull upward at the extreme edges, what happens? The extreme edges rise, but the bulk of the string remains behind (sags). Now, move your hands closer to the middle and pull upward, what happens? There is greater overall lift of the string, not just the extremes.

In character training for the local high school football team, I talked about "feet and courage," again words of wisdom from my college coach. The most important attributes you need to play any defensive position in football, especially linebacker, are feet and courage. Feet to get you where your read takes you; feet that are active and with a wide base; feet to keep driving through the tackle. Courage to trust your instinct on your read; courage to stick your nose in and make the tackle. How about we all live life with some more feet and courage? Use our feet to move us where we are called to be or need to be (as opposed to standing still): active and wide to meet today's challenges (as opposed to a statue or monument to the past) and feet to keep moving forward. Use courage to trust your heart, to be a better person and act. Use courage to do the right thing even when it is difficult.

How do we then grow as a society in today's world? Consider doing more of author Stephen Covey's Habit #5—"Seek first to understand then to be understood." Get down off our high horses, move our feet into the aisles and listen. Listen to the other side with discernment, as opposed to dismissing those ideas immediately. Consider Proverbs 18:15—"The heart of the intelligent acquires knowledge, and the ear of the wise seeks knowledge."

I heard Colonel Gary Steele speak a couple of years ago. He was the first African American football player at West Point. Imagine the feet and courage he had to achieve that accomplishment. He built his family mantra on an excerpt from the Cadet Prayer—"Encourage us in our endeavor to live above the common level of life. Make us to choose the harder right instead of the easier wrong and never to be content with a half-truth when the whole can be won." Be uncommon as opposed to common. Often, doing the right thing is more difficult, and half-truths will always catch up with you. Staying in our comfort zone often means accepting these half-truths.

The Station

At the kitchen table while I was in college, my dad shared with me an article called "the Station." It was written by Robert Hastings. Over thirty-five years later, I still have the original cutout from that evening's paper.

> Tucked away in our subconscious minds is an idyllic vision in which we see ourselves on a long journey that spans an entire continent. We're traveling by train and, from the windows, we drink in the passing scenes of cars on nearby highways, of children waving at crossings, of

cattle grazing in distant pastures, of smoke pouring from power plants, of row upon row upon row of cotton and corn and wheat, of flatlands and valleys, of city skylines and village halls.

But uppermost in our conscious minds is our final destination—for at a certain hour and on a given day, our train will finally pull into the Station with bells ringing, flags waving, and bands playing. And once that day comes, so many wonderful dreams will come true. So restlessly, we pace the aisles and count the miles, peering ahead, waiting, waiting, waiting for the Station.

"Yes, when we reach the Station, that will be it!" we promise ourselves. "When we're eighteen... win that promotion... put the last kid through college... buy that 450SL Mercedes-Benz... have a nest egg for retirement!"

From that day on, we will all live happily ever after.

Sooner or later, however, we must realize there is no Station in this life, no one earthly place to arrive at once and for all. The journey is the joy. The Station is an illusion—it constantly outdistances us. Yesterday's a memory, tomorrow's a dream. Yesterday belongs to history, tomorrow belongs to God. Yesterday's a fading sunset, tomorrow's a faint sunrise. Only today is there light enough to love and live.

So, gently close the door on yesterday and throw the key away. It isn't the burdens of today that drive men mad, but rather regret over

> yesterday and the fear of tomorrow. Regret and fear are twin thieves who would rob us of today.
>
> "Relish the moment" is a good motto, especially when coupled with Psalm 118:24, "This is the day which the Lord hath made; we will rejoice and be glad in it."
>
> So stop pacing the aisles and counting the miles. Instead, swim more rivers, climb more mountains, kiss more babies, count more stars. Laugh more and cry less. Go barefoot oftener. Eat more ice cream. Ride more merry-go-rounds. Watch more sunsets. Life must be lived as we go along.
>
> The Station will come soon enough. (Robert Hastings, "the Station")

My dad added something very significant to "the Station" essay. He related how important the passengers you meet on your journey are and how they add so much to your life as you learn their God-given talents and success stories. I remember Dad's Alaska cruise when he talked about the scenery and all the sights, but his enthusiasm grew when he started talking about the people he met—the fishermen and the village townsfolk. He found the most rewarding aspect of the trip was meeting and learning about their lives. He was genuinely interested in understanding who the people he met on his journey were and appreciating them as individuals.

The journey parable is also akin to an airplane flight. A pre-planned route is created for the trip and entered into the airplane's computer. In reality, the plane is exactly on its planned route a very small percentage of time as changes in air pressure, winds, traffic, and weather cause continuous adjustments to keep the plane headed for its destination. It is the journey and constant adjusting that is everyday life. Although we have a destination we are working towards and we create a plan to get to that destination, many things happen along the way to deviate us from that path. We need to adjust while keeping our eye on true north.

Accept the fact that nothing ever goes per your plan. Remember, if you want to make God laugh, tell Him your plans. Success is built on taking advantage of unexpected detours, setbacks, and embarrassments. Life serves them up routinely, so find joy in these messes.

> *I may not have gone where I intended to go, but I think I have ended up where I needed to be.*
> *—Douglas Adams,* the Hitchhiker's
> Guide to the Galaxy

Although the overall journey starts the day you are born, your life's conscious, purposeful journey can start whenever and can even restart. The past does not define the future, and all things are still possible. You need to have a destination in mind and a journey envisioned. You also need to realize the journey will likely change or better yet, evolve. Continually ask yourself if you are getting the most of what you can provide and are you making a difference. If the answer is no, then make a change.

> *Though no one can go back and make a brand new start, anyone can start from now and make a brand new ending.*
> *—James R. Sherman, Ph.D, American Author*

As you travel on life's journey, you make the choices, including how you want to travel. A person can be just as happy as he chooses to be, no matter the job he has, even a street sweeper, made famous by both Martin Luther King Jr. and singer Jimmy Buffett.

> *If a man is called to be a street sweeper, he should sweep streets even as Michelangelo painted, or Beethoven played music, or Shakespeare wrote poetry. He should sweep streets so well that all the hosts of heaven and earth will pause to say, "Here lived a great street sweeper who did his job well."*
> —*Martin Luther King Jr.*

> *A street sweeper came whistlin' by*
> *He was bouncin' every step*
> *It seemed strange how good he felt*
> *So I asked him while he swept*
> *He said "It's my job to be cleaning up this mess"*
> *And that's enough reason to go for me*
> *It's my job to be better than the rest*
> *And that makes the day for me*
> —*Jimmy Buffett, "It's My Job,"*
> *written by Mac McAnally*

The key to any journey is that you own it, and the key to a successful journey is that you know you own it. It is yours, so act and take control. *Learn from the past* but do not dwell on what was—keep looking ahead. Every day is an investment you make into your life. Once that day is gone, it is gone. It is a "use it or lose it" scenario. I love the scene in *the Lion King* where Rafiki hits Simba in the head with his stick. Simba says, "Hey, what was that for?" And Rafiki answers, "It doesn't matter. It is in the past."

In the book *Baseball and Philosophy* by Eric Bronson, there is a passage which discusses that in baseball, the intent is to get home. Yet, every batter starts off at home. "Home" in baseball does not count until you have left it then returned. Home does not become meaningful until you have taken the journey and experienced the risk that lies in front of it. You cannot score until after you have confronted the pitcher and those fielders who are trying to stop you.

I get a chuckle when I hear people make comments about the woes and pains of getting old. The alternative to getting old means your physical existence is over. I look forward to getting old, as old as possible. I plan on making a difference through it all. I also do not care how much my neck is bothering me or my knees ache; I will gladly deal with it. No doubt I will pay the price for living my earlier years. Football and sled riding banged me around pretty good, but I have no regrets on my journey.

> *Life is not tried, it is merely survived / If you're standing outside the fire.*
> —*Garth Brooks, Singer and Entertainer*

A good friend of mine shared with me the expression "that salvation is a journey not a destination." Some individuals speak of "being saved and accepting Christ" as if that then becomes the final act needed, a.k.a. the destination. While accepting Christ into your life in a greater way is momentarily humbling, this God-given grace inside of us is the beginning of the journey, so let us not just settle for this moment as the destination.

A great analogy shared with me by one of the students in our FCA Huddle is the surgery of an athlete to repair a torn ligament but then never following through with the physical rehab. The surgery healed the tissue, but you will never reach your full potential without making it part of the journey and thus the needed follow-through.

DO OR DO NOT, THERE IS NO TRY

The process of accomplishing something, striving to be accountable for outcomes.

Grit

Grit is defined as courage, resolve, strength of character, perseverance and passion for long-term goals coupled with a powerful motivation to achieve the objective. It is an overcoming of obstacles or challenges that lie within the path to accomplishment. Individuals with a prominent level of grit can maintain their determination and motivation over extended periods despite experiences with failure and adversity. Their passion and commitment towards the long-term objective is the overriding factor that provides the stamina required to "stay the course" amid challenges and setbacks.

- *Grit is better than Perseverance*, which is the steadfast pursuit of a task, mission, or journey despite obstacles, discouragement, or distraction. While perseverance is good, grit adds a component of passion for the goal.

- *Grit is better than Ambition*, which is the desire for attainment, power, or superiority. In contrast to ambitious individuals, gritty individuals do not seek fame or external recognition for their achievements. Ambition is often associated with a desire for fame. Unlike ambitious individuals, gritty individuals do not seek to distinguish themselves from other people but to obtain personal goals.
- *Grit is better than the Need for Achievement*, which needs feedback. Gritty individuals consciously set long-term goals that are difficult to attain and do not waiver from these difficult goals, regardless of the presence of feedback.

Society has stopped advancing grit as something to teach and grasp. Some parents think they are parents doing a good thing by going in and fixing their children's issues; therefore, teaching the child that he or she can't handle it. Schools have lowered the criteria for honor rolls and teach to a lower standard so more students "achieve accolades" to boost their self-image. We give everyone a trophy; we coddle our youth. Our country as a nation uses government bailouts.

We have stopped allowing our culture to suffer; thereby, forgetting this is often how one learns to be a success, maybe even survive. It is not politically correct to allow discomfort to ever develop. We are failing in developing the mindset to overcome any encountered or perceived problem. We remove failure and how to respond to failure; instead, we should embrace it as an inevitable part of life. We've become soft, and as such, more people get bitter than get better.

A study found the number one predictor of success is having the characteristic of grit—not grades, SAT scores, IQ, socioeconomic background or any other characteristic. Children who had the ability to stay focused on a goal, regardless of setbacks and obstacles and who weren't even concerned with positive feedback but just the goal, were the ones who experienced victory. A 2013 study also found that grit acts as a suicide resiliency factor by enhancing meaning in life.

Develop grit in the areas of your life that matter most—college, work, health, marriage, and faith.

Much of St. Paul's ministry was about grit. When he asked God to pull him out of a situation (which is much of what we pray for and then get mad when God doesn't like our treating him as if he is our bell hop), God answered Paul in 2 Corinthians 12:9, clarifying his role: "My Grace is sufficient." In other words, I, God, will give you blessings, not in delivering you but with Grit—with stick-to-it-ive-ness—with character. When criticized and questioned, Paul said in Philippians 3:13–14, "Forgetting what lies behind but straining forward to what lies ahead, I continue my pursuit toward the goal, the prize of God's upward calling, in Christ Jesus."

Grit goes beyond trying.

Finish

Some say the hardest part of any goal-oriented task is getting started. Even the great Mark Twain said, "Secret of getting ahead is getting started." I don't think so. If that were true, then why do people give up on their diet, exercise program, stop writing a novel, or quit a challenging work task? Because maybe it's the finish that's difficult. Many of us expect smooth sailing. However, there are always bumps in the road along with those unforeseen circumstances. Some of these things getting in the way are: discomfort, competing priorities, boredom, frustration, and even distraction. Embrace these bumps; don't run from them. If it were easy, everyone would do it. The goal should always be to finish what you started.

When he was at the University of Georgia, Coach Mark Richt introduced a concept known as "Finish the Drill." It grew into a motto for practices, workouts, and games. Good teams become championship teams based on their ability to finish strong. I recall two notable plays that stand out in NFL history because of "finishing." In the 2005 divisional championship game between the Patriots and Broncos, Ben Watson of the Pats (who played under Coach Richt at Georgia) tracked down and tackled Champ Bailey of the Broncos after a 101-yard interception return but one yard short of a touchdown. Then there is the Immaculate Reception with Franco Harris, who was in the right spot at the right time for history because he was doing what his college coach taught him—"finish the play."

Finishing builds:

- Perseverance. Adversity is a reality. Finishing strong trains the mind to push forward under adversity. We rise to meet the challenge. We create muscle memory to "keep going." Dogging it breeds quitting; finishing breeds toughness and perseverance.
- Focus. Failure occurs when people lose focus and gradually drift off the path. The ability to finish enables us to avoid temptation. Many people shoot out of the gate, and when faced with distractions, look for the effortless way out.
- Commitment to Excellence. A consistent effort to completion is the foundation of excellence. It creates a reputation of being dependable, faithful, and worthy of trust and admiration. These are the traits that an employer looks for in an employee, a spouse in their marriage, and children in their parent. Whatever you decide to do, set your mind to it and finish the drill.

Nehemiah was an incredible leader who rebuilt the Jerusalem wall in fifty-two days. Five times, men approached him and told him to stop. They tried to discourage him. But each time, they found him on the ladder working on the wall, and he simply replied in Nehemiah 6:3–9 that he was doing great work and could not be interrupted to come down because he needed to finish what he started. In fact, the chiding caused him to redouble his efforts to finish.

In the aftermath of the Boston Marathon bombing, three thousand runners and supporters finished what they started. They ran the final mile of the race one month later. Confidently, they used the slogan, "We'll get our finish."

Own the outcome and finish!

Success

Success in my eyes has never been measured by money, car, house, or how many possessions I have. Nor do I place my definition of success in the opinion others have of me. My measurements are how I am as a Christian, dad, spouse, coworker, neighbor, and in all my roles.

> *Our business in life is not to get ahead of others, but to get ahead of ourselves—to break our own records, to outstrip our yesterday by our today.*
> —*Stewart B. Johnson, Scottish Abstract Artist*

In doing some research for a football character presentation, I came across an interesting tidbit from our Founding Fathers. Both

George Washington and John Adams used similar lines in letters they wrote during the American Revolution:

> *No one can guarantee success. I can guarantee something better than success. We will deserve success.*
>
> —*George Washington*
>
> *It is not in the power of any man to command success; but you have done more—you have deserved it.*
>
> —*John Adams*

Thank goodness for the sake of our country they earned the success they were called to receive.

Success begins within and then comes outward. Believe you will be successful, visualize the success in your mind, create the feeling of success in your heart, and then allow your actions to deliver that success. In the summer of 1981, I had a conversation with my brother about the upcoming football season, and I shared with him that I believed in every game, there would be an opportunity for me to intercept a pass. I would need to be in the right place by having worked hard in studying films and reading the offensive setup. I would need to make the right decision and trust my judgments, and I would need to make the play (not drop the ball). In other words, I would need to put the toothpaste into the tube before it got squeezed. In the fall of 1981, I led the nation in interceptions. No one in college football at any school, at any level had more. I averaged almost one interception a game.

One day, sitting at the kitchen table when I was home for the summer on college break, my dad wrote the formula S=R/E on a piece of paper, Success (S) is equal to how Results (R) compare to Expectations (E). You can have wonderful results, but if they do not meet or exceed your expectations, you will not feel successful. It is the same in that you can have minimal results yet be considered a success if those results exceeded the expectations. If the expectation was for a team to win a championship and it does, it is the highest level of success for that sport. If they lose in the championship game, they will not consider the season a success. Yet if a team was a perennial loser and they won just five games, it would be considered a success.

Yes, setting low expectations and then achieving them easily could be a success. But that would be cheating yourself, society, and God on what you could possibly achieve. When you exceed lofty expectations, the success is even sweeter. Given the choice, I have always wanted to be on the team with the highest expectations.

> *Don't wish it were easier, wish you were better. Don't wish for fewer problems, wish for more skills. Don't wish for less challenges, wish for more wisdom.*
> —*Earl Shoaf, American Entrepreneur and Motivational Speaker*

A key to success is setting, clarifying, and communicating realistic expectations. These can be your own expectations as well as the expectations you have of others. You also need to know the expectations others have of you. In fact, the key to a happy relationship (business or even personal, especially marriage) begins with the communication of expectations. Having this conversation beforehand is a terrific way to avoid confusion and even disappointment. It can be disheartening when you feel you have achieved success (qualified for a bonus at work) only to learn you did not meet the expectations others (your employer) had of you. Make sure others are also clear on your expectations of them!

> *Great achievement is always, always, always pre-ceded by great expectations. If you don't believe in yourself and what you are trying to get done, you'll never accomplish anything special.*
> *—Kevin Constantine, Former National Hockey League Coach*

Success in life is more dependent on how long and hard you work than on talent. I have seen firsthand many successful people with less talent than others succeed because they worked harder and longer than their more talented peers. I have seen this in sports, in school, in business, as well as in relationships.

People can pretend to be committed to success; people cannot pretend to do the work necessary to achieve that success.

I love President Kennedy's speech to the graduating class of Rice University in 1962 when he said, "We choose to go to the moon not because it is easy, but because it is hard, because that goal will serve to organize and measure the best of our energies and skills." Doing things that are hard are needed and good for us. From the movie, *A League of Their Own*, Tom Hanks's character (Jimmy Dugan) tells one of his players, "It's supposed to be hard. If it wasn't hard, every-one would do it. The hard… is what makes it great."

Persistence does not mean doing the same thing over and over. Some people call that insanity; others will find it annoying. It can be having the same goal over and over. After Newton saw the apple fall, he began thinking about why it fell downward all the time. His persistence in asking the question "Why?" led to the discovery of the Law of Gravity.

> *You know what you gotta do when life gets you down? Just keep swimming... just keep swimming... just keep swimming, swimming, swimming.*
>
> —*Dory*, Finding Nemo

Choice

> *You have brains in your head. You have feet in your shoes. You can steer yourself, any direction you choose.*
>
> —*Dr. Seuss*

A key concept to really grasp is this aspect of "choice." You need to realize that you are in control of your thoughts, choices, and responses. Once you understand that you have control over yourself and the impact you have on what is going on around you, you gain a level of control over your life. You have ownership of yourself and are responsible for your success. Responsibility is the ability to choose your response. You can choose anything—be happy or sad, forgiving or spiteful, aware or unaware, etc.

I am often surprised at how novel this concept seems to be. Really, as a mature responsible adult (even a young adult), one should realize that they are in control of their thoughts, choices, and responses.

Listen to your language about choices. By using the right words about choices, you reflect your thought process and reaffirm that you do control your choices. Instead of making statements like "I can't," use the phrase "I choose to." People who always say, "I can't because…" are saying they don't have control of their life. Yes, you may have to choose work over play, paying taxes over going to jail, going to class over sleeping—but they are your choices. A song lyric from an oldies band called Rush goes "If you choose not to decide, you still have made a choice."

Strive to have integrity in the moment of choice. Choose based on your principles and values and not on your moods and conditions. This concept will grow with practice and conditioning. Like a drop step in basketball or a reach step that an offensive lineman in football takes, this step of mindful choice will take repetition to take root.

Not choosing to control your choices creates the "processionary caterpillar syndrome." Jean-Henri Fabre, a French naturalist in the early 1900s, experimented with processionary caterpillars, a type of caterpillar that blindly follows the one in front of it. He placed the caterpillars in a complete circle around the rim of the flowerpot, with the first one touching the back of the last one. Pine needles, the food of the processionary caterpillar, were placed in the center of the circle. The caterpillars began their procession around the flowerpot, one following the other in a circle. This went on hour after hour, day after day, for an entire week. In the end, every one of the caterpillars dropped dead of starvation. The one thing that could have saved them was only six inches away, but without purposeful thought or action, the caterpillars continued with a habitual routine that eventually killed them.

When you think about it, you have little choice on where you live or where you are when unexpected circumstances happen to you. However, you have total choice on how you live or how you act in response to circumstances. Along the same line, you never have total control on losing; however, you have total control on how you accept it and how you come back. Coach speak—"I don't care who we play, when we play, or where we play. I am only concerned with how we play."

There is a saying that goes "You didn't design the seas so you can't control the currents. You didn't design the boat so you can't make it unsinkable. But you can steer the boat through the seas." By not wasting effort on what you can't control, you have more focus (and available efforts) on what you can control.

> *What is important is not what happens to us, but how we respond to what happens to us.*
> *—Jean-Paul Sartre, French Philosopher, Writer, Activist*

Joseph in the Old Testament is the perfect example of choice: sold to slavery, servant to Potiphar, wrongly accused, imprisoned, yet he chose to maintain his integrity and deal with these circumstances. He then rose to become Pharaoh's right-hand man, put in charge of the whole land of Egypt.

There is a difference between gifts and choices. To paraphrase a commencement speech by Jeff Bezos, the CEO of Amazon: "Gifts are easy—God blessed us with our gifts. Choices are hard, because they are under our control. In the end, we are the sum of our choices."

> *It is not about what you are capable of. It is about what you are willing to do.*
> *—Mike Tomlin, NFL football coach*

In the above quote, capability is a gift; willingness is a choice.

Acknowledged ownership of the choices we make and of the consequences those choices produce creates personal accountability. You are accountable for your thoughts, choices, and responses.

> *Watch your thoughts, they become words. Watch your words, they become actions. Watch your actions, they become habits. Watch your habits, they become character. Watch your character, it becomes your destiny.*
> *—Frank Outlaw, President of BI-LO*

Be a thermostat, not a thermometer. The world needs "thermostats," those who take accountability and ownership of setting the temperature in the room as opposed to being a "thermometer" who just reports it. There is a significant difference. Thermostats are more accountable and take ownership.

"Accountability for Outcomes" as opposed to "Accountability for Actions." To produce breakthrough results, we need to take the accountability up a notch and make it about outcomes. Individuals need to be accountable for outcomes and to hold others to this same level of accountability. The focus shifts away from tasks and makes it about results. We could use more people focused on results, not actions. An attitude of "I own it, I will deliver, I can do it" with an effort to deliver the total required will serve you well. Just being accountable for actions can be like "checking a box" or going through the motions.

In the Gospel of Matthew is the Parable of the Talents (25:14–30), a favorite of mine and a great one about accountability. Servants were entrusted with talents, each according to his ability. When the Master returns, he wants to learn what the servants have done with the talents they received. What significance did they make of the talents they were given? Every year, I hear this gospel, but only after hearing it many times did the phrase "each according to his ability" strike a chord with me. It doesn't matter if it is one or five talents. The number isn't important; it's what you do with the talents that matters. Not everyone gets the same gifts. God has given each person a unique variety of gifts, and he expects each to use whatever gifts we've been given to the best of our ability. Luke 12:48 simply sums accountability emphasizing to whom much has been given, much is expected; and to whom even more has been given, even more is expected.

There are symbolic choices as to what guides your life—a compass, a map, or a clock. Are you guided by a purpose, a direction, or ruled by time? Decide what "True North" is on your compass. A compass always points north no matter what the situation; it is a natural law. Having a true north determined in your life acts like a compass when you evaluate your direction against it. A map provides a description which may be dated and inaccurate; you could have a map of Detroit and be lost in Chicago. Letting a clock rule your life means you may get things done quickly and succeed in a timely manner, but is it the results that matter most to you? Author Stephen Covey talks about being in a rush to climb the ladder of success, only to find that the ladder is leaning against the wrong wall. The compass is leadership, while the map and clock are management tools.

> *If a man knows not what harbor he seeks, any*
> *wind is the right wind.*
> —*Seneca, Roman Statesman*

In coaching youth soccer, I preached, "Don't just kick the ball; kick it with purpose." My intent being that the kicks would be passes or planned clearing attempts, but most of the time it was more like kickball than soccer. I am preaching the same thing with your daily life. Don't just live and exist; have a purpose for what you do.

> *Great minds have purposes; others have wishes.*
> —*Washington Irving, Writer*

Every child learns who Paul Revere was and about his famous midnight ride. Few people know who William Dawes was and that he made a similar ride that same evening. William Dawes was a tanner and a Patriot who rode in tandem with Paul Revere, one taking a northern route and one taking a southern route. Both were proclaiming the same news with the same fervor. Yet Paul Revere created more awareness in his ride and long remembered. Why? Paul Revere lived his entire life with a sense of purpose; he was involved and engaged in the community. He was a doer. People knew who he was because he related to them on many levels. William Dawes was a nice man and a good tanner, but that was the extent of it. He failed to connect with people; there was a lack of purpose in who he was.

Do Your Part

When someone says "have a nice day" or my wife tells me "safe travels," over the years my answer has become "I'll do my part" which can often get me weird looks (no longer from my wife, she chose to marry me). None of us have complete control over our circumstances so how can we possibly agree to have a nice or enjoyable day? I am not flying the plane nor driving the other cars on the highway, so all I can do is what I can do—my part—to travel safely.

In coaching high school football, it is important that all eleven players do their job and not someone else's. On kickoff coverage, I would have players leaving their lane to make the big hit or play, only to create a gap giving the opponent an easy advantage. Do your job and trust your teammates will do theirs.

In business, teamwork is essential, and business success occurs when individuals focus on doing their job in context with the overall needs of the company. How many times does someone solely care about their job and its results without regard to the impact it may have on others? Managing to make one's numbers on a spreadsheet look fantastic is like leaving your lane to make the big hit—it can turn out great, but it can also create undesirable circumstances. I have also heard more than a few times someone critiquing how they would do someone else's job better as opposed to focusing on their job.

I am a big fan of the *Die Hard* movies. Bruce Willis's character, John McClane, talks about being "that guy" as he finds himself amid these incredible situations. It falls upon him to be that guy and do his part. He states he rather not be that guy, but given the situation, he rises to do his part. Yippee-kai-yay!

Part of "Doing Your Part" is "Being Where Your Feet Are." You can't do your part of driving safely if you are texting; a football player can't focus on making the tackle if he is being blocked by a double-team; a salesperson cannot drive sales if he is concerned about inventory algorithms. The reason behind John McClane needing to be "that guy" is he is in the right/wrong place at the right/wrong time. It is where his feet are. As a man of honor, he'll do his part. In the words of Teddy Roosevelt, "Do what you can, with what you have, where you are."

Joe Moglia, the former successful CEO of Ameritrade turned head football coach (Coastal Carolina) as well as my first college football coach, does not have team rules. Instead, he has a philosophy: "Be A Man." It is about standing on your own two feet and learning to take responsibility for yourself, about being a great leader who has a respect for others and cares about other people in his or her charge, about always giving it one hundred percent of everything you have. In other words, "Do your part."

Scripture has many references to doing your part. I find Isaiah 6:8 a powerful reminder. We read where Isaiah says, "Here I am. Send me," when the Lord asks, "Whom shall I send?" Isaiah wants to do his part. I also really connect with Nehemiah. He was not a king or a prophet, just a regular guy who did his part. Despite ridicule and others trying to focus his attention elsewhere, Nehemiah stayed where his feet were, did his part, and rebuilt the walls of Jerusalem in fifty-six days. In fact, the Bible is filled with people doing their part, from Moses leading the Israelites out of Egypt to the Acts of the Apostles.

Sometimes we lose sight, thinking we need to be "keeping up with Joneses" or these days with the Kardashians. How can we do our part when we set a benchmark on someone else's part? In Galatians 6:5, "For each will bear his own load," is a reminder we will be judged on having done our part, not someone else's.

We keep looking ahead, wanting more, seeing the next import-ant thing. We tend to lose sight of what our role is along our journey, or should I say roles, because as we go through time, we take on various distinct roles, and some morph while we are in them. Too many men who have had children are not doing their part as a dad; some aren't even doing their part as a husband. Think about the wedding vows. You answer "I do" after being asked to accept your part in the marriage. You take an oath to "do your part."

If you have taken on the role, whatever that role may be, then you own doing your part. Wherever your feet are, be your best in that role. Per John McClane, "be that guy," or in Coach Moglia's vernacular, "Be A Man," or as Isaiah said, "Send Me."

Be faithful to where God has placed you and what path you are on for Him.

Failure

> *If you are irritated by every rub, how will your mirror be polished?*
> *—Rumi, 13th-century Muslim Poet,*
> *Theologian, and Islamic Scholar*

A mirror needs polish to be clear and to reflect the proper image. Without rubbing, the image gets distorted. The same way fire is needed to purify gold. Without it the precious metal is not so precious. A beautiful pearl is the result of an irritation from a grain of sand. Rubbing, fire, friction, and similar irritants are all necessary to produce better results.

If you don't allow yourself to be irritated, then you do not allow yourself to become better. If you don't expose yourself to the flames of failure, then you do not allow yourself to become purified.

I had the pleasure of hearing Jim Bearden speak a few years back. Jim is a decorated Vietnam War veteran and is now a business consultant, keynote speaker, author among other roles. He uses what happened on Hill 152 on July 12, 1968 to share lessons he learned that shaped his beliefs on leadership—learnings that were formed in the crucible of war. He was a 22-year-old second lieutenant who was dropped onto that hill by a helicopter to join a depleted Marine unit. That night, their unit came under an intense enemy attack, and he reacted in a personal manner by firing off shots from a 45-caliber pistol at the tree line in the distance as opposed to operating from his role as a leader to make sure the unit was effectively defending itself. Come morning, the carnage of the night before was visible, and he began to feel remorse thinking what if he had handled his leadership differently. A young Marine under his command prodded him into putting his grief aside for they still had a job to do. Jim says it was an epiphany for him, to make the choices essential to achieve what needed to be done. In his words, "Get over it and get on with it." Jim was made better by the fire he was subjected to.

My dad once asked me, after a particularly rough football game loss I had in high school, if I had done my best. I answered yes, that I had. His response was "then your best needs to get better, because it isn't good enough." There was no coddling there, a slap of reality that recalibrated just how much room there was for improvement. There is now a sign that hangs in the Westminster High School football locker room based on his words.

Every time you take the field, you are
vulnerable to being humbled when
your best just isn't good enough.

When it isn't good enough, then
your best needs to get better.

WE GET BETTER TODAY
FOR TOMORROW!

Why do we fear failure? There is no failure; one either succeeds or learns. The reality of "do not" from Yoda isn't a negative, just a fact.

Failure is an event, not a person.
—Zig Ziglar, Salesman and Motivational Speaker

History is littered with examples of success born from the ashes of failure:

- Henry Ford failed several times on his route to success. His first venture to build a motorcar got dissolved a year and a half after it was started because the stockholders lost confidence in him. He gathered enough capital to start again, but a year later, his financiers forced him out. Even though the entire motor industry had lost faith in him, he managed to find another investor to start the Ford Motor Company.

- Walt Disney did not start off successful. He was fired from an early job at the Kansas City Star Newspaper because he was not creative enough! His first company, Laugh-O-Gram, went bankrupt. Walt didn't give up; he packed up, went to Hollywood and started the Walt Disney Company.
- J.K. Rowling, the author of the Harry Potter books, like so many writers, received endless rejections from publishers. Her story is even more inspiring, because when she started, she was a divorced, single mom on welfare.
- Bill Gates, the cofounder and chairman of Microsoft, dropped out of Harvard and set up a business called Traf-O-Data. The partnership between him, Paul Allen, and Paul Gilbert was based on a promising idea but a flawed business model that ran up significant losses before it was closed. However, Bill Gates and Paul Allen took what they learned and avoided those mistakes whey they created the Microsoft empire.
- Noah McVicker devised a product that could clean coal residue from wallpaper in homes with coal furnaces. However, the transition from coal-based home heating to natural gas and the introduction of washable vinyl-based wallpaper decreased the need substantially and business dried up. McVicker's nephew, Joe McVicker, joined the company with the responsibility to save it from bankruptcy. They discovered that the wallpaper cleaner was being used by nursery school children to make Christmas ornaments. After re-releasing the product as a toy calling it "Play Dough," Joe McVicker became a millionaire before his twenty-seventh birthday.
- Milton Hershey failed in his first two attempts to set up a confectionary business.

-   H.J. Heinz set up a company that produced horseradish, which went bankrupt shortly afterwards.

Then there is the story of Matt Emmons. In the 2004 Summer Olympics in Athens, Greece, he had a significant lead when he entered the final round of the 50 meter rifle three positions competition. He hit the bull's-eye on his three shots but became puzzled as the automatic scoring system did not credit his shots. He called the judge over, and the target was pulled in to ascertain just what had occurred. It was untouched. No holes. The target in the next lane, however, had three extra holes—holes made by Matt's shots. His mistake cost him in the standings, and he finished eighth, no Olympic Medal. The story doesn't end there. Competitor Katerina Kurkova of the Czech Republic made it a point to introduce herself and offer her condolences. Less than three years later, they were married.

Scripture has many references as to the effects of trials and tribulations:

Not only so, but we also glory in our sufferings, because we know that suffering produces perseverance; perseverance, character; and character, hope. And hope does not put us to shame, because God's love has been poured out into our hearts through the Holy Spirit, who has been given to us. (Rom 5:1–5)

The God of all grace who called you to his eternal glory through Christ Jesus will himself restore, confirm, strengthen, and establish you after you have suffered a little. (1 Pt 5:10)

Blessed is the man who perseveres in temptation, for when he has been proved he will receive the crown of life that he promised to those who love him. (Jas 1:12)

See, I refined you, but not like silver; I tested you in the furnace of affliction. (Is 48:10)

The crucible for silver, and the furnace for gold, but the tester of hearts is the LORD. (Prv 17:3)

Getting rubbed, short changed, failing, etc. are all part of life and God's plan. Stop looking so hard at that event and look forward (and upward) using the experience to move onward.

Mistakes

Too many times, people hesitate to act, to decide, or want there to be more information or training or whatever before they make a choice. I look at it this way—if you act eighty percent of the time while spending twenty percent of your time analyzing about what to do and are only right half the time, that is a forty percent success rate (eighty percent x fifty percent); whereas, if you spend eighty percent of your time analyzing things and only twenty percent taking action and then are right all the time (which is highly unlikely), that equals a twenty percent success rate. By being more decisive, you are more successful. In this example, you are twice as successful. Act even if you don't know everything you should.

> *You don't have to be great to get started, but you have to get started to be great.*
>
> *—Les Brown, Motivational Speaker*

I have, hanging in my office, an excerpt from the *Wall Street Journal* titled, "Don't Be Afraid to Fail." The author is unknown.

> *You've failed many times, although you may not remember.*
>
> *You fell down the first time you tried to walk.*
>
> *You almost drowned the first time you tried to swim, didn't you?*
>
> *Did you hit the ball the first time you swung a bat?*
>
> *Heavy hitters, the ones who hit the most home runs, also strike out a lot.*
>
> *R.H. Macy failed seven times before his store in New York caught on.*
>
> *English novelist John Creasy got 753 rejection slips before he published 564 books.*
>
> *Babe Ruth struck out 1,330 times,*
>
> *but he also hit 714 home runs.*
>
> *Don't worry about failure.*
>
> *Worry about the chances you miss when you don't even try.*

The key thing about mistakes, whether you make them or they happen to you, is how they are handled. I determine how good a business or restaurant is by how they handle a mistake. Sometimes, how they handle the mistake gives you a better view of the business than if there was no mistake in the first place.

> *It is not what happens to you, but how you react to it that matters.*
> *—Epictetus, Greek Philosopher*

Mistakes are essential learning tools. It is acceptable to make mistakes. You cannot improve without making and learning from mistakes. Yet mistakes can also lead to difficult emotional reactions, such as frustration, disappointment, and anger as well as self-deprecating thoughts. These negative thoughts and emotions can paralyze a person and, like with an athlete, take them "out of the game" and make learning impossible because they are "trapped" in a negative emotional state. Choosing to learn from mistakes, accept feedback and positive criticism will allow you to grow and improve.

> *Mistakes are the growing pains of wisdom.*
> *—William George Jordan, American*
> *Lecturer and Essayist*

We never ask for our children to be perfect; we asked that they strive for perfection, knowing that in the effort, they'll become a better person and develop more of what God intended for them. The world's definition of perfection is something or someone that has no defects. From a Christian perspective, only God fulfills this definition. A better definition of perfection includes "completely suited for a particular purpose"—God's purpose.

> *There's no such thing as Perfection. But, in striving for perfection, we can achieve excellence.*
> *—Vince Lombardi, Hall of Fame Football Coach*

Vince Lombardi's quote notes that perfection measures our efforts and actions, and since we are human, we are flawed. It is excellence that measures who we are and our character.

> *We are what we repeatedly do. Excellence, therefore, is not an act, but a habit.*
> *—Aristotle, Greek Philosopher*

Mistakes are an indication that you acted. You did not sit back and do nothing. Mistakes imply actions that had results, results that allow you to learn and grow.

SPIRITUAL

Grace

There is an analogy between spiritual growth with grace and plant growth with sunlight, in that sunlight provides the power to photosynthesize and grace provides the power to do virtuous deeds. Grace is a way to live. It is a passing influence of God on the soul.

When a person works an eight-hour day and receives a fair day's pay for his time, this is a wage. When a person competes with an opponent and receives a trophy for his performance, this is a prize. When a person receives appropriate recognition for his long service or high achievements, this is an award. These are all man-made. There is a reward that comes from God—His grace.

But when a person is not capable of earning a wage, cannot win a prize, and deserves no award, that person can yet receive a gift anyway—God's grace. The grace of God does not have to be earned, it cannot be controlled, and you don't even have to deserve it.

If grace is out of our control, then let go and let God be in charge. Practice receiving and notice when things come to you without your effort. Grace isn't based on a scorecard; it just happens.

Below is my acronym for what I feel is the essence of God's grace:

Gratitude—a thankfulness for what we have as opposed to looking at what we don't have. God gave us what we need to live the life he has in mind for us. If we are not 6' tall or have an IQ of 150 or born into a rich family, it is because God decided he has other plans for us.

Respect/Reverence—a reverence for life, an awareness of what we are doing in respect to all things around us.

Accountability—a liability for one's actions in accordance with one's beliefs and God's standards.

Civility—a politeness and courtesy in behavior and speech. I find it alarming that many of today's hit reality shows are based on uncivil interactions between people. I also feel that texting, blogging, Facebook messaging, emails, etc. are allowing people to hide behind them and be uncivil. I would welcome going back to George Washington and his *110 Rules of Civility & Decent Behavior in Company and Conversation* that he wrote when he was sixteen.

Empathy—identify with another's feelings, emotionally putting yourself in the place of another. The ability to empathize is directly dependent on your ability to feel your own feelings and identify them. Stephen Covey discusses empathetic listening and how that improves mutual understanding (which helps with that whole expectations concept mentioned earlier), builds relationships, and creates trust.

Servant Leadership

This is a great parable I once read:

> *A man once asked God about heaven and hell.*
>
> *"I will show you hell," God said and took the man into a room. A large banquet table in the center was laden with every conceivable delicacy. The sight and smell of food were intoxicating. Around the table sat miserable, famished, and desperate people. Each was holding a spoon with a long handle. The spoons were strapped to their arms both above and below the elbow so that they could not bend their elbows and bring the spoons to their mouths. As a result, they were starving.*
>
> *"Now I will show you heaven," God said, and the man found himself in an identical room with an identical banquet table laden with a magnificent array of foods. Around this table were people equipped with the same long handle spoons strapped both above and below the elbows. Yet these people were smiling, happy, and well nourished.*
>
> *"Same table, same food, same spoons. Why are things different here?" asked the man.*
>
> *"Ah, but there is one important difference," God said in response. "Here in heaven, the people feed one another."*

Service, helping others, being altruistic without feeling any obligation to do so is a key piece of a rewarding life.

> *Everybody can be great... because anybody can serve. You don't have to have a college degree to serve. You don't have to make your subject and verb agree to serve. You only need a heart full of grace, a soul generated by love.*
> —*Martin Luther King Jr.*

Once when a Jesuit theologian was asked by a young man which books to read to help him strengthen his faith, he responded simply: "No books. Go out and help the poor."

Service should not be limited to structured situations or planned events. It needs to be part of your everyday life. It needs to be one-on-one and personal. By making it part of your principles, you touch more people in more ways, often without even being aware that you are doing something for someone else. It just becomes second nature, a habit. It also becomes a representation of how you treat people. Others can then be inspired by your actions.

A tremendous outcome of service to others is "peace at heart." By focusing on helping others, supporting one another, whether less fortunate or our peers, we can build a community of trust which will lead to a state of peace.

> *Peace is not something you wish for; it's something you make, something you do, something you are, something you give away.*
> —*Robert Fulghum, Author and Minister*

God gives us peace. No matter what happens, God is in control and with us always. But His incredible peace can only be given to those who know Him. In the Bible, the phrase "Don't be afraid" is the number one statement made. It is made as a command, not a suggestion. Our training should prepare us to meet any challenge. We may not overcome every opponent, but as children of God, we do not need to be afraid. God treasures us. He loves us very dearly and will take care of us.

All Christians are called to be servants, serving each other, following Jesus's example in washing his disciples' feet, and loving our neighbors as ourselves. Servant leadership is at the heart of Christian leadership.

When the disciples were requesting elevated positions in the coming kingdom, Jesus corrected their perception of leadership by pointing to the servant aspect of Biblical leadership. Jesus said, "You know that the rulers of the Gentiles lord it over them, and the great ones make their authority over them felt. But it shall not be so among you. Rather, whoever wishes to be great among you shall be your servant; whoever wishes to be first among you shall be your slave. Just so, the Son of Man did not come to be served but to serve and to give his life as a ransom for many" (Matthew 20:25–28).

Servant leadership is found in Paul's letter to the church at Philippi—"Do nothing out of selfishness or out of vainglory; rather, humbly regard others as more important than yourselves, each looking out not for his own interests, but [also] everyone for those of others. Have among yourselves the same attitude that is also yours in Christ Jesus" (Philippians 2:3–5).

Servant-leaders model integrity, where their thoughts, words, and actions flow from a consistent desire. One of the biggest reasons for leaders losing the respect of their followers is that they lack true integrity where their private lives and thoughts do not match their public statements or that they are inconsistent, adopting principles that are popular and appropriate to the moment, rather than sticking to their underlying, but potentially unpopular, principles. That is losing their "gap control."

Hockey teams play what they call a "gap-free" defense. The concept is to minimize the gap between you and your assignment (an opposing player). The bigger the gap, the more space and time the opponent has to operate and thus more detrimental to your chances of succeeding. This gap-free concept applies to how we live. Are there gaps between beliefs and behaviors? The more space and time in the gaps, the more likely for failure in living the life you should. Be gap-free.

Congruence is defined as "no gap between intent and behavior," a match between values and actions. Your values and your integrity bring you to a decision. It might not be an easy decision nor even a correct one in other's eyes. It will be the right decision as it is based on your core values and not based on opinions, convenience, or external pressures of others.

Servant leadership is not a style of leadership, but rather, it relates to the motivation behind a leader's thoughts, words, and actions. Leaders can fit any of the leadership styles and still be very much a servant-leader. Servant-leaders are not leaders based on their position or leadership role, but rather lead according to their calling, vision, and principles.

Leadership is intentional influence. Intentional influence is a deliberate and purposeful ability to affect change and make a difference. A true test of leadership is that somebody follows voluntarily. You can be a leader of a process or movement (someone like Martin Luther King) as well as be an everyday person that chooses to lead in the moment (think Rosa Parks). Both are just as critical.

> *If your actions inspire others to dream more, learn more, do more, and become more, you are a leader.*
> *—John Quincy Adams, President*

Success or failure as a leader does not come down to whether one is charismatic, visionary, or inspirational. It comes down to whether, at the end of the day, people behave in ways that improve results. Period.

General Eisenhower would demonstrate the art of leadership with a simple piece of string. He'd put it on a table and say, "Pull it, and it will follow wherever you wish. Push it, and it will go nowhere at all." It's just that way when it comes to leading people. They need to follow a person who is leading by example.

> *Leadership: The art of getting someone else to do something you want done because he wants to do it.*
> *—Dwight D. Eisenhower, President and General*

Compare Dorothy and the Wizard as leaders.

- The Wizard defines his role with power and authority using fear, barking out orders and comments, hiding behind a structure.
- Dorothy was a peer. She built a team based on relationships, common goals, and compassion where everyone reaches their potential.

The opposite of a servant-leader is a serve-*me* leader. This type of leader emphasizes his/her "command" or mandate rather than his/her example. He/she is pushing the string. Although the servant-leader has the authority and power to demand, he/she chooses instead to motivate through kindness and to educate by example. The serve-*me* leader prefers to lead by mandate rather than example because serving by example involves two actions which the serve-*me* leader wants to avoid at all costs.

First, leading by example provides a frequent reminder that the leader is "just like us." It diminishes the hierarchy distinctions which a serve-*me* leader seeks to expand and maintain. The serve-*me* leader desires those under his leadership to consider him/her to be above their level. Second, leading by example means getting one's hands dirty. Cleaning toilets, washing dishes, changing diapers, and a host of other tasks are activities which the serve-*me* leader believes are "below him/her." In contrast, the servant-leader remains willing to take on the most menial tasks.

Driven vs. Called

While I was preparing my college hall of fame acceptance speech, this concept of being "called" as opposed to being "driven" came to the forefront of my mind. Growing up I had heard so often about needing to be driven to succeed. "Determine what you want and go get it." That was not my style, yet I felt successful. I began to connect the dots of my life's journey. I was not driven to attend Lafayette or to even play college football. My dating my eventual wife, my career choices, and even my coaching high school football were not things I doggedly pursued. They all emerged on their own in their own way. The more I reflected, the more the answer became obvious to me—God has had a hand in it all, calling me to live the life He dreamed for me.

Driven and called are very different. Driven people feel the need to own everything. They believe they are the sum of what they have or possess. Their language is based on *I, me, my*. Called people feel they are a steward for their talents and that they are a sum of what they give and what they stand for.

Driven people tend to have an ego. Ego is Latin for *I*. Egotists thrive on self-importance, being vain. Their ego is based on image, conquests, and compensation. Their decisions are based on what benefits them first. The two biggest ego motivators are fear and pride. Fear causes you to protect your self-image/self-interest; pride causes you to promote your self-image/self-interest.

The alternative to ego replaces fear and pride with confidence and humility. Confidence is not self-confidence but God-grounded confidence, and God-grounded confidence does not rely on performance or on the opinion of others. Humility is the "lack of vanity or self-importance." To be humble is to be devoid of self-pride, to be neither arrogant nor assertive. Ego can also stand for "Edging God Out."

People with humility do not think less of themselves; they think of themselves less. They do not deny their power; rather, they recognize it passes through them, not from them. God tells us that our job is to humble ourselves and His job is to exalt us. If we reverse the roles and do His job exalting ourselves, then He will do our job for us and humble us. It is one of the most powerful laws of the universe.

"Be Moonlight" has become one of my favorite metaphors in this area. The light we show forth is like the light of the moon, which has no light of its own but merely reflects the light of the sun. The moon is no more the creator of its light as we are of the light we reflect. We need to reflect the light of the Son of God.

Doing Thanks

Giving thanks is expressed in words. We value a person's good manners or deeds by the words "thank you." Many were taught from the first time they could talk to say "thank you." Saying thank you is important, but there are times when saying thanks isn't enough; doing thanks is needed and is essential to Christian behavior.

We can say thanks to those who help us, or we can pay it forward and help others first. We can say thanks to those who planted flowers, or we can plant more flowers ourselves. If we have good health, we can use that health to help someone who has failing health. If we are good with children, we can offer to babysit for a frazzled parent or coach a youth sports team. If we are blessed with a little extra time, we can visit someone who is homebound or in a nursing home. If we have a good education, we can help to educate someone else—by tutoring a struggling student, by listening to a child read, by contributing to our high school or college scholarship fund, or by donating a book to our local library. If we have life experiences that we learned the hard way, we can share those experiences with others to help them on their paths. Let thanks be always on our lips and in our deeds. In short, doing thanks is the best way of giving thanks.

The story in the Bible regarding Mary and the anointing at Bethany (John 12:1–8) is an example of doing thanks. Jesus had just raised Mary's brother Lazarus from the dead. Mary could have written a thank you note or, if she lived today, sent an Edible Arrangement of fruit flowers. However, for Mary, giving thanks in any traditional way was not going to be enough. She felt compelled to express herself by "doing thanks"—lavishing on Jesus a gift that, as Judas was quick to point out, could have been put to better use: helping the poor. Hers was an extravagant act of love: pouring out a whole pound of "costly perfume" (one year's wages) to anoint Jesus's feet. Lazarus was more than a brother to Mary and Martha and a dear friend to Jesus.

If the women were dependent on their brother as the male head of their household, his death would have had devastating consequences for them. Women with no male relatives to speak on their behalf or to look after them often ended up homeless or were forced into prostitution to survive. With their brother's second chance for life, both Mary and Martha did indeed have much to be thankful for; raising Lazarus was an act of mercy and compassion. Her response to Jesus's compassion was her extravagant act of love—pouring out the best of what she had to give. Judas saw it as a waste, but Jesus saw it for what it was.

"Doing thanks" can often be as simple as doing a little bit more.

In Genesis 24:10–20, there is a fitting example of going above and beyond, "doing a little bit more," as we serve others. Some scholars call it "the Rebekah principle." Abraham had sent his servant off with all the riches and resources at his disposal to find a wife for his son Isaac, as was the custom in that time. Upon arriving at the city of Nahor, toward the end of a long day of travelling with a caravan, a young lady named Rebekah is at the town well drawing water for her family. The traveler poses a simple request for a drink of water, and Rebekah responds by saying she'll not only fulfill his request but give his ten camels enough water until they have finished drinking also. Keep in mind how much water camels drink! By sharing from her abundance, she was doing thanks and paying it forward. So, when the camels had finished drinking, that man bestowed to Rebekah rings and bracelets of gold, and then she becomes the wife of Isaac. A wonderful transformation occurs in her life that was born out of her attitude and mindset of selflessness to a stranger.

Unity

The definition of unity is the state of being one, combining all its parts into one. Whether we're talking about a marriage, a sports team, a company, a church, or even a nation, unity is a foundation for achievement.

The song "If We Are the Body" by Casting Crowns came up in my song list shuffle play. It is a good song that touches on the desired unity of the Church, where those not in the inner circle are also included. I like the analogy of the body as a good one for unity. Unity is something that is living; it is not mechanical. The human body is an organic unity. It consists of many parts: toes, fingers, hands, feet, legs, eyes, ears, etc.; it is not a collection of parts put together such as an automobile or a house.

As a football coach, I know that a winning football team is another example of unity. It is a combination of a diversely talented individuals from diverse backgrounds working together harmoniously for the good of the whole. No inner circles and no hidden agendas.

Creating unity is not so much a necessary program but an environment. Unity cannot be coached like a skill set or learned in a webinar. However, coaches and leadership can create the proper atmosphere and seed the growth of unity. Successfully create this type of environment and there you find highly driven teams.

Unity happens:

- When there is the concept of "abundance mentality" compared with "scarcity mentality"
- When team members care more about the vision, purpose, and health of the organization than they do their own personal agenda

-   When group members share their gifts to one another's benefit
-   When each person on the team can clearly see how their personal vision and effort contributes to the overall vision and success of the team
-   When you weed out the negativity that sabotages far too many organizations
-   When leaders are committed to and engaged in the process of building a united, winning unit which commands their focus, time, and energy

A scarcity mentality mindset operates so that in order for someone else (even a teammate) to win, then I must lose. This mentality says there is only so much success and I need to get my share. This leads to selfish behavior. The abundance mentality operates so that the "success pie" continues to expand and the slices get bigger and that everyone can share in the success. It is a win-win attitude. People with the abundance mentality are better friends, teammates, and colleagues as they help everyone win.

Unity also happens through open communication, accountability, and trust. Unity happens when there is love, *philios*. There is no room for negativity with this love.

Philios means close friendship or brotherly love in Greek. It is one of the four types of love in the Bible. It is the most general form of love in the Bible, encompassing love for fellow humans, care, respect, and compassion for people in need. Love and hidden agendas cannot coexist. A great scripture reference is 1 Peter 3:8—"Finally, all of you, be of one mind, sympathetic, loving toward one another, compassionate, humble." What I like about the scripture is the note to have harmony with "unity of mind" and a humble mind. It does not say that we all need to look and behave the same.

Our football team has used the slogan "One Heartbeat" for years. It is more than just a motto; it truly is the essence of who we are as a team. To have one heartbeat, there must be a higher calling than being just a collection of players. The higher calling requires respect, compassion—*philios*. For a unified company, there needs to be a strong corporate culture, a culture based on more than stated values and mission statements. It's essential that all members of a team or company are moving with a shared vision, focus, purpose, and direction. A truly shared vision and purpose needs to have respect for fellow employees (i.e., love) at its core. Unity is love of a spouse, love of a teammate, love for brotherhood and sisterhood.

> *We come to love not by finding a perfect person,*
> *but by learning to see an imperfect person perfectly.*
> *—Sam Keen is an American Author,*
> *Professor, and Philosopher*

I am thankful my wife follows the advice of that quote! To see an imperfect person perfectly, plug the word *spouse, teammate, business colleague, neighbor,* etc. in for *person.* Love requires intentional effort, as does unity—neither will just happen.

However, it's not easy to bring people together. Agendas, egos, politics, power struggles, negativity, poor leadership, mismanagement, and a lack of vision, focus, and purpose all prevent a team from uniting and performing at their highest level. There are hundreds of potential negative forces and factors that can sabotage unity, and it only takes a few to accomplish the disruption. The good news is that there are many examples of unified teams showing us it is possible.

The default behavior for human beings is to think in terms of their own "inner circles." If you work in a small department in a big company, you are naturally going to identify most closely with your immediate colleagues. It is easy to love those whom you agree with, those whom you know—harder to love strangers than your fellow man. Cliques, another name for inner circles, within teams and organizations poison the environment such that unity cannot take root.

One definition of unity I read includes the phrase "the absence of diversity." I disagree with that completely. There is a need for diversity in unity. Think of the human body again. The parts do not look alike; they do not function alike, yet they are all important, needed, interdependent, and all work toward the same end. Some of the parts are within the body and are unseen but, nevertheless, very important. Each part of the body is integrated into the whole. A football team has skilled players who most often get the attention, but without the interior linemen doing their job, these skilled players can't be successful. How successful would a sales rep be without a customer service group?

Unity is not uniformity, nor does it require assimilation. Those "extreme" perceptions by some people on either side of the social spectrum are doing more harm than good and driving us as a nation away from unity. The mindset that we all need to be alike to be united is elitist, while at the same time, the mindset that I lose my identity when I become unified is narrow-minded. We need to embrace diversity as part of unity, and we need to recognize that the sum of all parts working cohesively together is larger than that of the whole, and the value of integration is paramount to achieving goals and positive outcomes. Being "additive" does not destroy objects in the current blend nor does it destroy that which is being combined. Integrate the best of what each party offers. Unity does not mean we must all become exactly alike as our variety gives richness to our existence.

Results of history in the world when it comes to forcing unity within nations include:

- Nations with ethnic and racial uniformity, not diversity
- Boundaries reflected by language, religious, and ethnic homogeneity
- Diversity within a nation considered a liability, not a strength
- Ethnically homogeneous countries felt more stable and secure
- No tolerance for someone of Japanese descent being fully accepted as a Mexican citizen or vice versa
- Nazi Germany incorporation of all the German "Volk" into one vast racially and linguistically harmonious "Reich"
- Deadly force enforced to keep the factions in line. Think about the Soviet Union, Rwanda, and Iraq with Shias and Sunnis

America has been history's exception. It began as a republic founded by European migrants that, due to the definitive logic of a unique Constitution, steadily evolved to define Americans by their shared values, not by their superficial appearance. Eventually, anyone who was willing to champion the core values of the Constitution became an American. America is a collection of different personality types, various economic levels, variety of opinions, and very different backgrounds (culture, environment, experience). But, as Americans, there are certain basic, fundamental things we share and must agree on. These things tie us together. However different we may be in a variety of secular ways, there is a spiritual and practical unity we enjoy based on this common bond.

America is the great melting pot. *E Pluribus Unum*—from many to one. Some more "politically correct" minded people are now arguing the semantics that, as opposed to being a melting pot (where you are assimilated and lose your identity), America needs to be a "salad" where the individual maintains its identity yet adds to whole. No matter what cliché or analogy we choose to use, we must preserve the ideals that made America successful as the unifying "one heartbeat." When we are together, there is no greater nation, and the same applies to teams and organizations. There will still be problems, but collectively, they will be solved much easier than individually. Abe Lincoln said it best: "A house divided cannot stand among itself."

The need for unity is driven by competition. In sports, it is the desire to win the game, have a successful record, or win the championship. In sales business, it is the need to make a profit, hit earnings targets, and grow the business against your competition. In marriage, it is the resolve to excel as a couple, to build a loving household, and to honor the sacrament. In a church, it is the drive to honor God and achieve eternal salvation. In a nation, it is to defend our nation's sovereignty and maintain our freedom. Think back to WWI and WWII, 9/11, the Great Depression—these were trigger points to rally the nation and drive unity. Through unity, we overcame hardships and defeated enemies. Today, we need a unified nation more than ever as we fight among ourselves, against ISIS, and against terrorism to regain our place in the world. It seems as if we are far from being united. Let's start with more love in our everyday lives.

Be it a marriage, a football team, a company, or a nation—success is based on unity.

Renewal

Make sure you take care of yourself and are recharging your own personal batteries. Analogies include making sure you put gas in the car, oil in the lamp, and a sharp edge on the saw. Stephen Covey's

7th habit is called sharpening the saw. His point is that if you are too busy sawing to take time to sharpen the saw blade, the blade gets dull, and it takes more effort to accomplish the same task, and eventually, the blade gets so dull, it becomes impossible to cut.

> *Give me six hours to chop down a tree, and I will*
> *spend the first four sharpening the axe.*
> *—Abraham Lincoln, US President*

Renewal needs to be in all phases of life—physical, with exercise and rest; mental, with reading and writing and listening; social, with service and family time; spiritual, with prayer and meditation.

I have come to celebrate Candlemas Day, February 2nd which, long ago, was the basis for Groundhog Day. There is a renewal process associated with Candlemas Day. Its purpose is to clean your body and soul. St. Paul notes that our body is the temple of the Holy Spirit and should not be defiled. Many people spend their health looking for wealth then, later in life, spend their wealth looking for health.

Too many segments of today's society are spiritually undernourished. Materially, scientifically, and technologically, we are accelerating every day, but spiritually our society remains an infant. Society will only grow in spirituality as its individual members seek this growth. With pious spirituality, individuals influence everyone they touch and contact in a positive way. To realize how an individual can cause this spiritual growth within a society, remember that Jesus only started with twelve.

> *The Lord works from the inside out. The world works from the outside in. The world would take people out of the slums. Christ takes the slum out of the people, and then they take themselves out of the slums. The world would mold men by changing their environment. Christ changes men, who change their environment. The world shapes human behavior, but Christ can change human nature.*
>
> *—Ezra Taft Benson, Religious Leader and Secretary of Agriculture*

Having your spirituality as part of your everyday life is important in gaining that renewal. Make it a part of your core, and it will serve you when you need it most, which will often be unexpected.

> *To pray only when in peril is to use safety belts only in heavy traffic.*
> *—Corrie ten Boom,* the Hiding Place
> *Author and Rescuer of Holocaust Jews*

Did you know that religious people with peace in their hearts live longer? Numerous studies have been done over the years that show people with strong religious beliefs, as well as regular attendance at worship services, live longer, live healthier, and recover from surgeries or illnesses quicker. One study performed on elderly residents showed that those who were weekly worshipers were more likely to live on their own and be free of disabilities. People with a sacred religion at their core typically have better habits (don't smoke, exercise more), have social support networks, healthier marriages, and lower levels of stress. People with peace in their hearts maintain a healthy version of happiness.

Faith

The most revealing statement I made during college about my faith was soon after the football season in the fall of 1981. Because of the incredible success I enjoyed, I started fielding questions about the season I had. The quick answer was that age-old expression you hear a lot from athletes, "I was in the zone," but then my answer became "God wanted to play some college defensive back, and he chose me." The physical ability I had was God given; I knew that. Skills and talents are gifts from Him. However, during this season, it was more than physical talent. The Holy Spirit was present and taking me to a higher level of play. My mental ability and instinct were higher than they ever were. That season, I saw routes developing, had better anticipation, and instinctively knew what the offense would be doing next.

Back then, I was not very open about my faith, so my "God playing defensive back" was said with some humor and was the extent of a witness or testimony to my faith. In hindsight, God was working with me in a more subtle way with His timing. During college, I was exposed to the Fellowship of Christian Athletes, even leading the huddle in my senior year. I attended mass with my college girlfriend, who eventually became my wife, which was an incredible foundation for our relationship. These were little stepping stones building the path to where I am today—helping with a high school football team, character coaching, serving as the FCA huddle coach, plus serving on the local FCA board. All these have been a catalyst for the Holy Spirit to do even more with my faith.

I continue to walk my walk with my Lord. It is my personal walk, to be ultimately judged by Him. I would guess the biggest struggle is the pace, how much of it I am controlling when it needs to be His pace. It is true that we are called to walk, not run or sprint. Although this "on again/off again, two steps forward/one step backward, all over the place" pace just may be the pace He sets for me.

> *Life is not about serenely walking down the middle of spick-and-span streets. It's about veering to and fro, bouncing off the guardrails, and then overcorrecting. But you can't correct a course until you've taken to the road!*
> —*Tom Peters, the Renowned Business Author*

The road I have taken is unique, and it is mine, one that I was called to take. It blends my faith, family, football, business, my love of quotes, and just everyday life together. To steal a line from the Rascal Flatts song, "Bless the Broken Road": "It's all part of a grander plan that is coming true." I plan to continue to walk my broken road, focus on learning as I go and not racing to the end result. Enjoying my walk and sharing it through devotions and witness with the belief that it serves a purpose, His purpose.

The Appetizer and the Entrée

Did you ever attend a dinner event and realize you missed out on some great appetizers because the servers were focused elsewhere in the room? Or have you experienced cold or half cooked appetizers and been really bummed? Then there are also those times where you over ate on the appetizers, and it spoiled the meal.

Did you ever, after the round of appetizers, have the most wonderful meal you ever could have imagined, a meal that made you forget there ever were appetizers? What if you knew ahead of time that the meal was going to be so spectacular? Would you have been upset at the lack of appetizers or even if they were not so great? Would you have overindulged on the appetizers such that you missed the main entrée?

I attended a funeral for a dad of three boys who were high school classmates of my youngest daughter. He was not much older than me. I heard the familiar conversation that he died too young (he did!). Around the same time, I also had been recently reflecting on the plight of a graduating senior who, although born with a genetic disorder, is one of the most beloved students in the school. Then there was a newscast of the six-year darling of a little girl dealing with a heart transplant, where the chance of survival was slim at best. Add to those items that I still have the obituary of a college football teammate who passed away, leaving behind a beautiful wife and three daughters, at the youthful age of thirty-seven (Oh, but for the grace of God go I).

Life really can be unfair, or so it seems. Some of us are born into situations better than others. Some of us make mistakes and stand in the corner of the room where the appetizers never reach. Some of us physically don't "measure up" against others. But in reality, we are dealing with the appetizers here. Did we get enough appetizers? Did we get the better ones right out of the kitchen, or were they cold? Our focus is on what is coming before the main meal.

The entrée is ahead of us, and it is the most wonderful meal ever beyond our comprehension and imagination. The key point is that we know about this incredible meal ahead of time, and yet, we still worry about the appetizers. Instead of focusing on the entrée and making sure we are prepared to come to that table with our hands clean and our hearts pure, we pay too much attention to the number of appetizers and if we got the best ones. Some of us are gorging ourselves on appetizers such that we will miss the entrée. Some of us are refusing to share our appetizers.

Yes, let's enjoy the appetizers that are a part of our life. Better yet, let's pay attention to those around us at this event, enjoy their company, and prepare to enjoy the entrée.

Coach Mahr's Blessing

Godspeed is an expression from an old Middle English phrase *God spede* which means "may God cause you to succeed." It is also an expression used with the intention of a personal blessing and true concern for someone to successfully accomplish or complete a challenging task, typically someone about to start a journey. Its most famous usage was on July 16, 1969, when Apollo 11 blasted off from Cape Kennedy, Florida. Three astronauts, Neil A. Armstrong, Michael Collins, and Edwin E. "Buzz" Aldrin Jr. were atop a 363-foot tall, 7.6-million-pound thrust Saturn V rocket thundering towards the Moon. They were the last words heard from launch control.

I use the expression often. This book is the perfect opportunity to impart my blessing as you journey onward, and I wish you to succeed.

Paying blessings forward is a form of doing thanks. I am one to whom much has been given, so I know that much is expected of me. Taking the opportunity to share these thoughts and life lessons is, in some small way, my washing of feet and serving others.

Build your success story that is personal to you, then share those blessings forward.

ABOUT THE AUTHOR

Bob Mahr, as an author, is answering a calling to share his faith and experiences as a business leader, athlete, coach, and father. Bob takes his mission from Luke 12:48: "to whom much has been given, much is expected." He has learned that making a difference in business, athletics, communities, and family rely on the same common threads woven together.

Bob is a director of a multimillion-dollar division for a National Supply Chain partner and has held leadership positions for large multinational corporations as well as small companies. He is a member of his college's athletic hall of fame, was a three-year starter on the football team, and earned professional tryouts in the NFL and CFL. He has been a volunteer coach for over fifty teams at every level from recreation soccer, AAU and high school basketball, high school and college football, as well as Special Olympics volleyball. He is an active member of the Fellowship of Christian Athletes as a board member, campus huddle coach, and character coach. Most importantly, he is a devoted husband to Vicki and father of three adult daughters, all becoming citizens in today's society.

He feels fortunate to have discovered something special and has a mission to share with others.

CPSIA information can be obtained
at www.ICGtesting.com
Printed in the USA
LVHW092303110719
623866LV00001B/80/P

9 781641 918947